PAINTINGS FROM THE WILD

PAINTINGS FROM THE WILD

THE ART AND LIFE OF
GEORGE McLEAN

BY DAVID LANK
Special Introduction by Bob Kuhn

THE BROWNSTONE PRESS

CANADIAN CATALOGUING IN PUBLICATION DATA

Lank, David M., 1937–
Paintings from the wild

ISBN 0–919275–04–4
1. McLean, George, 1939–
2. Painters – Canada – Biography.
3. Animals in art.
4. Birds in art.
I. McLean, George, 1939–   II. Title.
ND 249.M35L36   759.11   c81-095028-6

Printed and bound in Canada.
Distributed by John Wiley & Sons Canada Ltd.

Dedicated to my mother, VIOLET

MCLEAN, and my wife, HELEN, for

their goodness and for all the good they

did me

GEORGE MCLEAN

CONTENTS

Colour plates   ix

Drawings   xi

Introduction   xiii

The Art and Life of George McLean   3
   The Man   5
   The Traditions   13
   The Art   24

Paintings from the Wild *with notes*
by George McLean   33

Selected Bibliography   145

LIST OF
COLOUR PLATES

Red-tailed Hawk Mantling, 1977	35	Mountain Goats, 1979	111
Bald Eagle, 1976	39	Otter with Pond Lilies, 1979	115
Canada Geese and Goslings, 1978	43	Pronghorn Antelope, 1976	119
Crow on Beech Limb, 1971	47	Red Foxes and Beech Tree, 1977	123
Sketch of Eastern Bluebirds in Fog, 1976	50	Sketch of Fox and Hare, 1969	126
Eastern Bluebirds and Cornflowers, 1977	51	Red Fox Running, 1977	127
Evening Grosbeak, 1973	55	Snowshare Hare, 1980	131
Golden Eagle and Prey, 1970	59	Tiger with Kill, 1976	135
Sketch of Owl and Eastern Grey		Wapiti, 1979	139
Squirrel, 1979	62	White-tailed Deer with Fawns, 1978	143
Great Horned Owl and Jackrabbit, 1978	63		
Peregrine Falcon and Meadowlark, 1970	67		
Sketch of two Red-tailed Hawks, 1979	70		
Red-tailed Hawk and Starlings, 1979	70		
Red-tailed Hawk on Maple Limb, 1974	71		
Red-winged Blackbird and Cattails, 1972	75		
Ring-necked Pheasant, 1976	79		
Sketch of Grouse Eggs, 1981	82		
Study of Forest Floor, 1976	82		
Ruffed Grouse and			
Jack-in-the-Pulpit, 1971	83		
Ruffed Grouse and Second Hardwood			
Growth, 1971	86		
Ruffed Grouse Displaying, 1981	87		
Short-eared Owl Landing, 1979	91		
Charles in the Grass, 1975	94		
Charles on the Woodpile, 1969	95		
Study of Trees, 1977	98		
Sketch of Cougar, 1977	98		
Cougar Reclining in Tree, 1978	99		
Golden Lab Retriever, 1978	103		
Lioness and Vultures, 1975	106		
Young Lioness, 1975	107		

*Medium: Casein on masonite coated with
white acrylic gesso*

LIST OF DRAWINGS

Raccoon, 1964   5
Black Bear, 1964   8
White-tailed Fawn, 1964   9
Study of Great Horned
    Owl and Jackrabbit, 1973   16
Black-crowned Night Heron, 1976   23
Crouched Lynx, 1972   24
Leopard, 1980   25
Cougar Reclining, 1977   26
Red-tailed Hawk, 1974   70
Cougar, 1977   98
Red Fox Running, 1980   124
Red Fox Walking, 1968   125
Wapiti, 1965   138
White-tailed Doe Reclining, 1964   142

Medium: Pencil or Charcoal

INTRODUCTION

The pace of the evolution of realism in animal painting has been dreadfully slow, compared to other areas, for one reason above all others. Those who have sought to paint wildlife have for centuries struggled to truly understand their complex and varied models. Creatures that served man or consoled him, such as dogs, cats, horses and others domesticated or confined for his use, were the first to yield to man's persistent scrutiny and study. Slowly, with the advent of zoos, the less accessible members of the wild kingdom began to assume more recognizable form on the canvas and paper of artists in the more disciplined cultures of the West, though of course, primitive people had anticipated this awakened interest by many thousands of years.

Only in this century have we who draw and paint and model animals been able to see into the subtleties of animal motion by means of fast-shutter still photography as well as slow-motion cinematography. So now, with the door to a more complete understanding of our subject open to us, we can vest our subjects with life and motion and character to the full extent of our abilities. Whether that new confidence is translated into works that deserve to survive is up to

each of us. It is the proposition of this book that George McLean is among the most intense and devoted of the present day coterie of wildlife painters and that his work will endure.

I first met George when I was plying my trade as an illustrator and he was a brash, young fellow haunting the zoos and museums within his reach in eastern Canada. After a few letters back and forth, he came down and spent a brief time in my studio. It was the first of many visits to our place. After his marriage to Helen, they would both come to call, and it was soon obvious to my wife and me that the merger was one of George's wiser decisions. Always he would bring photos or reproductions of recently completed work. And so I've had the pleasure of seeing his paintings evolve into the carefully wrought creations they are today.

It is not my proper function in this introduction to go into detail about my young friend's method. Nor will I describe this work or that. I must comment, however, on his total absorption in the planning and execution of each piece that gets past the doodle stage and becomes a serious effort. McLean's principal concerns are, it seems to me, the use of space and attention to detail. Because of his painstaking preparation and then his slow patient application of textures, be they fur or feather, the work goes slowly and the output is less than many collectors would

wish. But tricky ideas and facile solutions are not George's way. Rather, his is the more probing, testing quest for the profound truth of a subject faithfully and lovingly painted, valid as to setting and animal behaviour, and elevated above the mundane by a sure sense of design.

I think it would be fair to say that through those annual visits I had a hand in George McLean's early development, if encouragement and an occasional comment on his work, completed or in progress, can be so described. Later, my own mentor, Paul Bransom, though by then an old man, became his counsellor and friend. Neither Bransom nor I, however, was George's true spiritual ancestor. That distinction belongs to the great Swedish painter, Bruno Liljefors. It is this man, working his wonders well into this century, who was to draw McLean into his orbit. Since Liljefors, much honoured in his day, is generally regarded by today's wildlife painters as number one, one can hardly quarrel with my friend's gradual drift into his magnetic field. I don't mean to suggest that McLean is a carbon copy of the master, far from it. But he is as drawn to the rocky outcrops and pine forests of his native Canada as Liljefors is to the lonely barrens and coves of his northern home. Each, being an artist, speaks in his own voice.

I believe George McLean will probably continue his lonely voyage of discovery, always searching for simpler and truer ways to capture the essence of his subjects. The love will continue to be evident and perhaps some of the detail will fall by the wayside. It is often thus. The viewer likes the quick fix that fidelity to the outside of things provides. The artist learns early or late that you have to go past the surface, however lush or elegant or bizarre that surface is, to get at the nature of the creature beneath. But George, being George, is not likely to change dramatically. He will probably continue to caress the surface of his paintings much as he would, if he could, caress the creatures themselves. One would as soon expect Andrew Wyeth to treat a greyed old section of weathered barn with detachment as assume that George will no longer choose to work his meticulous magic on the breast of a Great Horned Owl. That is unless his own inner need dictates a gentle swing away from his present fond treatment of detail and texture.

Such a shift may be too slight to be noticed. No matter. I for one will settle for more of what I've already seen. If the surprise is not in the treatment it persists in his choice of subjects. For George McLean's view of the wild world is always interesting and always illuminating. And so I can look forward to paintings that have yet to go through the painful process of gestation and birth, some-day to emerge from the farmhouse-studio and assume their place among the solid, enduring examples of our shared special craft. It is a field, incidently, which is attracting more and more practitioners – but not many who will be remembered. George McLean is making sure that he is among those who will be.

Bob Kuhn
Roxbury, Connecticut
June 7, 1981

PAINTINGS FROM THE WILD

THE ART AND LIFE OF GEORGE McLEAN
by David Lank

Propped up on the easel a large painting was in progress. A Great Horned Owl was swooping, wings extended and talons bared. Below, to the left, an Eastern Grey Squirrel hurtled through the air, its tail and limbs trying to counteract gravity for a controlled escape. The rest of the board was lightly pencilled with a grid of squares within which a tangle of branches and pine trees would emerge to form an incredible forest of muted greens, blues, greys and browns – all from the same palette that had given birth to the owl and the squirrel.

The painting was hardly complete, and yet it was already a nascent masterpiece. The owl was palpably alive. The subtle colours in the incredibly real featheration implied a sense of great detail where very little actually existed. This was the real feather pattern, born of impressionism, not of the microscope. The wings interacted with the air and gravity, and the feathers responded with their own inherent physical characteristics. The eyes transfixed the falling squirrel with concentration, not theatrics.

The squirrel was alive. The eyes and ears were alert. The fur broke under commands sent by the muscular little body and was pushed and spread by the wind. From a few steps back, the squirrel seemed perfect; from up close a few faint grid marks still showed through the casein paints. 'Hell,' grumbled George McLean, 'I've got to work him up a lot more. I've only put in six or seven hours

work on him.' Another 80 or 90 hours work and the finished painting would bring together the key elements already fully explored in the small painted study.

Without publicity, one of the world's greatest wildlife paintings would go straight from the easel to a discerning and demanding expert collector. There would be no fanfare. George McLean would remain little known outside of a limited circle of artists, art historians, scientists and critics whose own experience and exposure permit them to appreciate his true talent and importance. The overriding purpose of this book is to broaden that circle.

It is distressing and not a little discouraging to read or hear the indiscriminate praise heaped on illustrations of no merit whatsoever. No one artist can be called 'the best' until the passage of time has allowed his works to find their proper place in the context not only of his contemporaries, but also in the rich tradition that has come before. To state otherwise is ignorance. What can be said, however, is that never has there been a greater number of talented artists devoting their lives to animal art. Similarly, it can be said that a handful stand out above the rest.

One of that handful is George McLean. Working unobtrusively in southern Ontario, he is producing some of the world's finest art. It is true art; it happens to deal with the living world. It is an art that springs from a passionate caring for wild creatures, from a determined respect for technique that can only come with a lifelong commitment, and from a surrender to self-discipline which

leaves no brush stroke, no dab of colour, no element in the composition to chance. Technically, artistically and intellectually, it is art on its highest plane.

To his fellow professionals, his paintings are known, admired, even envied. To the public at large, McLean remains less than a household word. With only six or seven major paintings a year, he is likely to remain so. That his work is so eagerly sought by the most knowledgeable collectors is a testimonial to his art, not an indication of a demand based on his notoriety. His is not a market created by exaggerated promotions. This prompts the second major reason for this book. Back in the 1880s, Joseph Wolf, one of the most significant wildlife artists of all time, could have been voicing the frustration of today's best painters when he said: 'The thing I have suffered from is the general ignorance about my subjects, not only with purchasers, but also with hanging committees, and my greatest difficulty has been to fathom the depth of this ignorance.' This ignorance extended, as it does today, to many members of the scientific community. Wolf added: 'Some ornithologists don't recognize nature – don't know a bird when they see it flying. A specimen must be well dried before they recognize it. It is impossible, for instance, for a mere museum man to know the true colour of the eyes.' True, scientists have been guilty of dismissing as useless anything other than detailed engineering drawings, usually in profile. Art, according to them, was inaccurate, and inaccuracy was the mortal enemy of science. But artists have been for centuries equally myopic, sneering at science and treating her simplest laws with disdain. The second reason for this book is to try to lessen the ignorance about animals in art. Hopefully, with increased knowledge, there will also be an increased demand and appreciation for excellence.

Wildlife art has not enjoyed the reputation it merits. Indeed, there have been whole epochs when the portrayal of natural subjects, alive and for their own sake, was frowned upon by virtually every serious critic, shunned by museum curators, spurned by patrons, and worse, considered by leading artists as a pursuit below their dignity. Many great artists have even boasted of having absolutely no knowledge of animal anatomy or behaviour and defended their lack of expertise by claiming that animals simply did not count other than as decorative elements in their masterpieces.

That this unhappy state of affairs persists in many quarters even today is all the more incredible because animal art is as old as art itself. Every age has had artists who revelled in the beauty of nature, and a continuous chain has been forged by men and women of genius and sensitivity from the cave paintings of Lascaux and Altamira of 20,000 years ago right up to the present. Again, it was Joseph Wolf who could have been describing the prejudices of today when he caustically observed: 'If you paint a dead linnet or red poll, it is admissible to the Royal Academy. If you paint it alive, it is a transcript of an object of Natural History, unfit for exhibition.' It is indeed an irony that far more technical and artistic talent is required to capture the essence of a living creature than of a corpse.

Animal art is as woefully misunderstood today as it was a century ago when Wolf etched the critics in acid. Art has all too frequently been defined and evaluated by the amount of detail. Understandably, museum curators and hanging committees fear to encroach on the displays that more rightly belong at the annual meetings of game conservation groups. Mallards exploding off a pond and other hackneyed subjects are better suited to calendars and the lids of chocolate tins, but the influence of sporting 'art' among the buying public has had an impact on the overall animal art market. It has tended to drag even fine animal art down to the lowest common denominator.

With the advent of television, high speed photography and the conservation ethic, an unprecedented number of people have been exposed to wildlife vicariously or through guided tours. Few are the people who have spent hours or days enduring the true environment of the animals to gain an accurate sense of community with wild creatures. Frequent visits to the zoo are a pale substitution for field experience, and movement frozen in a coffee-table book bears little relationship to movement in reality. The veneer of knowledge about the natural world has made thousands of people feel competent to judge animal art whereas they would, rightly, shy away from passing judgment on any other art form.

The more complex the art and the artist, the more knowledge a critic should bring to bear on any evaluation. George McLean and his art, therefore, pose a challenge, as they are both very complex. To understand his art it is important to understand the man himself and the rich tradition from which he springs.

THE MAN

Raccoon

You reach McLean's house by driving through miles of his paintings. Gravel and pavement alternate along the Ontario concession roads that have been imposed on rolling hills by a surveyor's order, not by the logic of the land. It was mid July. The first crop of hay was in and giant yellow bales, eight feet in diameter, lay strewn about the stubbled green fields like so many gargantuan spools. Split cedar fences and dry stone walls marked off the inheritances of generations and added a sanctuary for birds and small mammals where tractor and hoe could not intrude. Cornflowers stiffly spread their powdery blue petals towards the sun. Asters and wild sweet peas cascaded down graded slopes by the hundreds to mingle with the floral doilies of Queen Anne's Lace along the drainage ditches. A thousand shades of green resolved into the pointillism of a million wildflowers.

Marmots, like huge four-footed woolly caterpillars, rippled back into a hedgerow, and a raccoon lay dead a few inches from safety. A skunk posthumously scented the air while a short-tailed weasel dashed by on urgent business. The telephone wires were so many musical lines: the notes were swallows, kingbirds, meadowlarks and Red-winged blackbirds. Goldfinches undulated through the air, and overhead a massive black Turkey Vulture scanned the fields on upturned primaries. Crows flapped silently up from the road, and flickers by the score flashed yellow as they dove for cover. A Song Sparrow sang, and a Kestrel hovered in air made drowsy with the hum of insects.

Silos thrust suggestively skyward, and the sun glinted through the haze off the metal roofs of barns. Past red-bricked gingerbread Victorian farmhouses, past clustered graveyards, past fields where small pyramids of cedar were beginning to reclaim the abandoned land, past Walter's Falls with only a young boy and a small dog visible from among its 200 inhabitants – the road passed through the raw material that I had come to know in the paintings submitted for the now legendary *Animals in Art* exhibit of the Royal Ontario Museum in 1976. In the intervening years I had seen McLean's work only infrequently but each time I was astounded at his talent and maturity. Driving through Ontario farmland was therefore something of a pilgrimage for me. The road kept changing colours on the map and soon was reduced to two ruts with a median of grass that swished against the underside of the car. A hundred miles north of Toronto in the region of Owen Sound, George McLean's home might be called isolated. In fact, for the first two years, he and his wife, Helen, had to snowshoe in a mile from the nearest roads in winter. But the isolation from the city has not separated him from the world he has captured so inspirationally in his paintings. The 50 or so species of small birds and mammals that share his land have been returning to this country just below Lake Huron's Georgian Bay for a millennium and had claimed it as their own long before the settlers of Walter's Falls either named them or their town. McLean could not find the animals in an urban setting, so he came to nature, and brought his easel with him.

Walter's Falls is too small to be on any but the largest maps. A dam impounds Walter's Creek every night to build up a head of water behind the mill for the day's work. Every day, therefore, the creek that flows through the bottom land on McLean's property rises and falls, creating a rich blend of meadow and forest, swamp and tangles. The land has been worked for generations, but now is reverting to nature. The wildlife, the flowers, the trees, the luminosity of the atmosphere, the gnarled and weathered cedar stumps, the vestiges of man and the surrounding farms that are still being cultivated, the changing seasons – all these provide an endless source of material for the artist's eye.

As a child, McLean used to escape from the toughest of inner-city districts in Toronto. An occasional visit to his grandparents in the country fed his fascination for the outdoors. In 1939, when he was born, his family situation was unenviable. Economic insecurity is sometimes easier to sustain in the country, or so his mother thought. So in 1950, the entire family moved to the Caledon Hills, 50 miles from Toronto. The rural experience did little to improve the family's lot, but during the two years before returning to the city it did provide McLean with the environment in which his lifelong passion for wild creatures took root. He was, by his own description, 'as wild and as much a part of the outdoors as the animals themselves.' He skinned the animals he trapped and discovered the similarity in structure of birds and mammals. This callous handling of death was not intentionally brutal. Rather, it was the only way open to an impoverished youth to slake his thirst for knowledge. Books, to George, were few and far between.

As a man, McLean has not hunted or trapped for years, and yet he feels closer to the animals, not only physically but spiritually, than he ever did. In fact, the only skins he has today for study purposes come from the road kills brought to him by friends and neighbours.

Just how soft he has become is well illustrated by his love for crows. 'You've never seen an unhappy crow living wild. They're a mess, they're scavengers, they're really intelligent, and above all they're successful. The people around here knew I loved crows, so I wasn't surprised when a neighbour drove up asking me if I wanted one. I figured it was another road kill. But when he opened the trunk there was a wounded crow, battered about in the dark and looking truly unhappy. That was the only sad crow I've ever seen. Can you imagine doing something like that to a crow or any wild creature? I didn't take the crow. I would have had to kill it, and I just couldn't bring myself to do it.'

Such compassion might seem strange for a person whose street-smart early years were geared for self-preservation. In short, his background could have provided ample justification for a different sort of feeling and a totally different sort of career. For some of his schoolmates, it did. For George, it steeled him with an inner strength and a tough exterior to match. Despite the strength and toughness he nurtured an unbreakable softness. 'You're right,' he growls. 'No one loves animals more than I do.' This compassion is not maudlin; it is a compassionate acceptance of nature and her rules. 'I don't make my animals cute, I try to make them real,' he explains. 'I don't feel sorry for the rabbit being chased by the hawk. Hell, he'll probably get away. They usually do, which is why there are a lot more rabbits than there are hawks.' This kind of sentiment, rather than sentimentality, cannot come from books. It can only evolve from an education in the field that is never ending.

There was, however, a more conventional education as well. At age 17, he discovered Toronto's Central Reference Library. Here there were files on artists, reproductions of their work, and books. The intellectual and emotional impact was profound. He was attending Toronto's Northern Vocational School, studying commercial art, and looked forward to the weekly visits to the Royal Ontario Museum for drawing classes. Greek pottery left him cold, but he was captivated by the wildlife exhibits. There was no question in his mind, even at a relatively early age, that someday he wanted to paint animals exclusively.

The sketching led to a chance conversation with a security guard who arranged an unannounced introduction to Terry Shortt, the dean of wildlife artists and the then-head of the museum's art department. Ushered into the office, McLean saw Shortt working on the skin of a Northern Loon. It was a bittersweet revelation. 'It hit me like a ton of bricks,' he recalls. 'To realize that places and people like this had existed all along and I hadn't known about them made my whole body ache with frustration. I knew that all I wanted to do was to get through high school so that I could get into the museum to learn my trade. I know now that that would not have been the place to do it, but I felt a desperate need for the security I thought a museum job would give.'

The Museum did not offer him a job. He remembers the crushing disappointment and even resentment, but in retrospect he feels that the greatest thing that ever happened to his career was that no job materialized. He never would have lasted and would surely have made powerful enemies he could ill afford. His growing up had not honed his social skills, and he thrived on the impatience of youth. An awkward turn of phrase could surely be misinterpreted. He was intellectually starved, and he demanded satisfaction. His hunger for knowledge begged answers and responsiveness far beyond what most people could or were willing to give. His insistence on more was frequently equated with aggressiveness. The museum administrators, the fellow staff members, and probably the visitors would soon have dismissed him as an enormously talented loner. The security he sought would have to come from within.

Terry Shortt did, however, introduce McLean to the works of Carl Rungius and more importantly to those of Bruno Liljefors, the incomparable Swedish genius of whom much more will be said. Today, McLean states quite candidly that 'no one has had a more profound effect on the way I see a picture than he did.' McLean had studied some art history at school, but from the vantage point of animal art, the great influences of his career, Liljefors, Léo-Paul Robert, John James Audubon and others were not discovered in the classroom. He had learned about Monet and Constable but was still too inexperienced to appreciate their full significance in terms of colour, composition and technique.

Of far greater immediate impact were two artists whose work McLean kept noticing in various publications. Jack London's *Call of the Wild* thrilled McLean partly for adventures beautifully told, but largely because of the fabulously evocative illustrations done by Paul Bransom. This master had also produced material for such leading American magazines as *Saturday Evening Post*, so McLean had access to Bransom's strength of line, colour and composition. (Not insignificantly, a copy of the first edition of *Call of the Wild* inscribed by Bransom to McLean lies in the studio as a prized possession.) Bransom had been a youth of 17 when he had done those illustrations, so, despite the doubts of his art teachers, McLean had proof that there could be a career in animal art for a young man.

Bransom, as it turned out, was the mentor of another artist whose large, forceful game animals snarled their way through powerful landscapes in the pages of many outdoors and hunting magazines, the primary publications in which animal art of any type could be found. McLean did not even know

Black Bear

how to pronounce the artist's name, but Bob Kuhn was his idol. Just as a young aspiring bird painter, George Miksch Sutton had brazenly written to the brilliant Louis Agassiz Fuertes for criticism, so a young George McLean wrote Bob Kuhn, and their correspondence turned into a friendship and a professional respect that has continued to grow over the years. The early letters are now lost, but in them Kuhn encouraged McLean to devote his life to painting animals, and above all to being himself. 'Mostly he gave me a kick in the pants,' McLean smiles, 'but he also gave me constructive criticism. When someone with more experience says something, you can't understand it at the moment. You catalogue it in your head, and later on, as you gain experience yourself, you suddenly realize what he was talking about, and just how right he was. Bob did that for me.'

Kuhn influenced McLean's early days primarily in sketching anatomy, muscles and gesture. The drawings from that period were hard and sculptured, but that overzealous line was essential for a young man mastering his craft. As Fuertes had written to Sutton: 'No outside critic can be as valuable to you as you yourself, provided you keep honest with yourself, and are not afraid to see the weak places in your work and labour to cure them.' In a later letter to Sutton he added: 'Don't get discouraged, and draw, draw, draw!'

No one taught McLean to draw, but only with constant repetition could the lines soften and allow the artist to emerge from the draughtsman. From his earliest years he scribbled on everything and anything, and most often his efforts were directed towards wildlife. What his formal training really gave him was an understanding of how to create certain textures, as well as an introduction to art history. The rest was intuitive and repetitive. McLean's passion for wildlife poured out through the pencils and crayons in the form of countless sketches done at the zoo where he laboured over poses, perspectives, the physical aspects of fur and feather, and the muscles and bone underneath. The few sketches that remain provide a fascinating insight into the development of the young artist. Compared to his mature work they seem sculptured rather than drawn. But as the hand became surer and the artist more knowledgeable, the rigidity turned to fluidity. The detail receded as the essence advanced. McLean devoted his time to something that far too few artists today bother with: he learned to draw.

White-tailed Fawn

His talent was now obvious, but a career in wildlife art was considered a naive dream that would quickly fade before the seductive crackle of a dollar bill. Earning a living in commerical art is difficult at the best of times; a career as an animal artist would end disastrously.

One of his earliest commissions was a series of small vignettes, some in colour and others in black and white, for an extremely attractive catalogue published for the North American Arms Company in 1961. Unfortunately, the company went bankrupt before the catalogue was distributed. His first exposure to the larger world was stillborn. A person from Seagram Distillers then approached him for a series of paintings of large game, a commission that McLean was proud to accept. By a twist of irony, the two artists who had painted the previous two series were Paul Bransom and Bob Kuhn.

McLean's first major opportunity came with the invitation from Dick Hersey, the art editor of *Weekend Magazine*, one of Canada's largest newspaper supplements, to supply eight paintings. The reproduction was all that could be expected on newsprint, but the talent could not be denied. Of greatest importance, at that juncture in his career, was the fee, which covered his modest living expenses for a whole year and even permitted McLean to purchase materials as basic as a light for his draughting table. It also provided the funds to allow him the time for more firsthand field work. Commissions came in steadily thereafter, but the income was just enough to keep him on a treadmill.

To move off dead centre, McLean needed a patron. Bruno Liljefors found the freedom to create only after Ernest Thiel put him on salary. Benvenuto Cellini had a succession of Renaissance popes, and every king and princeling had his court painter. George McLean found M.F. (Budd) Feheley, a well-known Toronto critic, dealer and collector. They struck a bargain that gave the young artist sufficient funds to be able to concentrate on his art. No limits or minimums were imposed on his output. He was to use the time and the independence to improve through study, practice and experimentation. For the next 11 years, Feheley represented McLean and was the single most important influence on the artist's professional life. Says McLean today, 'Of all the dealers I've ever had Budd is far and away the most knowledgeable. He was a very professional person who came along at the right time, took me off the streets, and gave me security. But of greatest help, he gave me tough professional criticism. He also tried to teach me the hardest fact of life, namely, that you have got to look after yourself because ultimately no one else will.'

Within this working relationship McLean developed quickly. He gave up all thought of being an illustrator. 'Bransom, N.C. Wyeth, and so many others,' he explained, 'were turned on by the stories that were told by others. I just wanted to tell my own stories.' His paintings now began telling stories of those endless hours in the field learning to see and trying to understand the habits and the habitats of the creatures. Alongside of this expanding data bank, McLean began to discover by trial and error what the paints would do, how they reacted with one another and what textures could be achieved.

The results were spectacular, but they remained basically hidden. McLean's art was too advanced, too subtle for the mass market, and too complex to be differentiated from superficial art by the popular galleries. He was, in effect, ahead of his time. Moreover, McLean was not easy to promote. He was not a shy man, by any stretch of the imagination. He remains forceful in his manner and his words. 'A diamond in the rough,' he was called.

At the conclusion of the arrangement with Feheley, McLean associated himself with Chris Yaneff of Toronto, owner of the Yaneff Galleries and of his own advertising agency. It was Yaneff's love of art coupled with his marketing skills that took McLean's work to a broader audience.

Intuitively even those with the most cursory knowledge of wildlife and art felt the power and the aesthetics of McLean's work, but too few were the buyers and the critics who could understand, let alone demand, the distinction between a painting which contains an idea and a mere representation of a bird. The media and the promoters turned their spotlight on the paint-every-feather school. McLean's frustration, alienation and loneliness deepened.

His career had reached a crisis stage. 'I had only a few loves,' he explained, 'and absolutely paramount among them was my art. Without my work I could not have existed. Everyone I knew was in relation to my work. I have never painted a painting for anyone but me. But, if Bob Kuhn or Budd Feheley or someone else whose opinion I valued came to see a work, I got nervous. I knew that if they praised me, they weren't apple-polishing. It would be because they felt so strongly about my work that they just had to say so. That was the only kind of compliment that I respected, and the only kind of praise I treasured. But if I was prepared to accept their true compliments, then I had to be prepared to receive their negative criticisms too. In the kind of shape I was in, negative criticism would have just about done me in.'

No one, however, understood his art or himself as well as his wife Helen. 'She was the other great love of my life. She was totally supportive and supplied the balance I so desperately needed. When things got to be almost unbearable she would sit in the studio beside me as I worked and would read to me for hours on end. Together we pulled through.'

One of McLean's closest friends described the relationship between George and his wife. 'George has a fanatic inner restlessness. But time and time again he would tell me of Helen's steadfastness, of her quiet and indomitable support. But don't think for a moment of her as a passive mirror of George. Helen has achieved her own distinction, teaching school, taking night courses to complete her bachelor's degree, and finally winning a university gold medal on graduation as top student.

'George's emotional support has come from Helen, and from his mother. Despite the sometimes bizarre circumstances of his early life, he drew from his parents, and latterly draws from Helen, the kind of base from which he can achieve.'

McLean not only survived and flourished. Above all he has not compromised his art to pander to the fads of the galleries or market. Mindful of Kuhn's early advice, he remained true to himself. This was not an easy path to follow.

In the 1960s, animal artists had two strikes against them. The first was that only dead art was really acceptable. A rabbit suspended by a foot could be masterfully painted, surrounded by old books with a candle reflecting in a crystal goblet. This was worthy of the great museums. The same rabbit, alive and breathing, was considered inferior.

But the second strike had been thrown specifically by the New York dealers and museum people of the 1950s who had been the self-appointed and totally unquestioned arbiters of what constituted good art and good taste. What they pronounced good among contemporary art was without exception abstract. Realism was anathema and detail boorish. North American wildlife artists, so firmly a part of the Audubon tradition, were therefore doubly burdened because they dealt with animal art *and* realism. The towering genius of Andrew Wyeth changed all that, as he was the first major contemporary realist to be accepted by the art community and helped give animal artists the opening they needed.

Twenty years have gone by, and absolutely microscopic realism has ruled. As the slide towards almost idolatrous detail continued, the level of animal art produced in North America sank so low that the 1960s and 70s were dubbed in some quarters as 'The Golden Age of Dross.' There was glitter but few riches.

Meanwhile, in Europe, wildlife artists following the great traditions of Robert and Liljefors were leaving their American contemporaries far behind. When the best the world had to offer was brought together at the Royal Ontario Museum's *Animals in Art* retrospective, the contrast was shocking. The pendulum of detail had swung too far, and the purveyors of even the most trite clichés grew restive. The good artists had mastered their idiom and they really chafed to expand beyond it. They realized that detail *per se* was nothing more than a technical exercise.

Artists with an obsession for detail frequently do not know what to leave out, and others who have never mastered the handling of detail do not know what to put in. Only the true naturalist/artist instinctively knows where to strike the balance in order to capture the essentials. Liljefors, for example, once painted a masterpiece of an Eider labouring over the troughs of a curling wave. The bird was depicted as it would be seen from a distance of about 100 feet. With the movement of the flying duck, the light, and that distance, it would be impossible for a human observer to see the eye. So Liljefors left it out. This lack of detail did not in any way diminish the essence of the Eider.

Detail by itself is not a valid criterion for art; in itself it is neither good nor bad. If excessive detail is cited as proof of greatness, the artist has an obligation to ensure that the detail is at least correct. Similarly, a critic should know what he is talking about. To prove a point, Terry Shortt once painted a fine portrait of a bird with two left feet. None of the so-called experts spotted the 'error.' Had Reubens painted his nudes with two left feet, we might wonder what the reaction would have been.

The work of G.H. Ford is useful in illustrating the extremes to which the fetish for detail was taken. In the 19th century, Ford produced absolutely faultless paintings of snakes and other reptiles. The draughtsmanship was perfect. Every renticulation on the skin was precise, and the interesting problems of perspective along the sinuous bodies were handled in a manner mathematically above reproach. The finished result was a scientifically accurate portrait of a snake with every single scale properly placed and drawn. But the work was devoid of art. There are plenty of Fords around today, only they paint every hair rather than every scale. The technique and the talent are basically the same, and yet the avian products of these skillful delineators are praised as art. The sole difference between scales and feathers is one of subject matter. Art, therefore, has become defined by the subject. Feathers are more pleasing visually than scales. To claim one as art and not the other is a perversion.

No one is more aware of the proper role of detail than McLean. He places great importance on pterylography, the systematic study of the arrangement of the plumage upon which the beautiful precision of the markings of a wild bird so much depends. This should not be confused with microscopic detail; it is rather an understanding of pattern based on a knowledge of detail. The featheration and pattern on the plumage of his unfinished owl gave the impression of an abundance of minute detail, but on closer examination, only the essence was captured. Queen Victoria's favourite animal painter, Sir Edwin Landseer, bluntly told an art class that they would never paint a decent picture until their eyesight started to fail. Joseph Wolf, at age 75, claimed he could paint a better picture then than he could at age 40. 'I saw too much,' he explained.

There is another more important kind of detail. This is the detailed knowledge of how the various animals and birds interact not only with one another, but also with their habitats.

This knowledge is gained unexpectedly. McLean runs four miles a day, winter and summer, in his heavy Kodiak boots, mostly

THE TRADITIONS

as a way of burning off some of his boundless energy. It also gives him a chance to see and learn. 'One day I came across the remains of an ermine. Only the tail and hindquarters were left. The hawk or owl didn't care for the musk glands around the tail, so he left them. The other two quarters and the torso were gone. I haven't used it yet, but,' he adds, pointing to his head, 'I've salted it away in my catalogue file.'

This unrelenting gathering of new information is an outgrowth of McLean's fundamental belief that 'no one has the right to call himself an artist if he first can't call himself a "fond observer." This was Canadian artist Thoreau MacDonald's thinking. He is a great artist. Liljefors and Robert were fond observers and I feel that I am too.'

Others have observed, too, and McLean realizes that studying the artists who have come before is important. To understand George McLean it is essential to review the rich if little known traditions of animal art that have spanned the centuries.

Artists have thrived since prehistoric man adorned his caves, but the scope for expression was limited until the coming of non-nomadic civilization. Political, military, mercantile, academic and religious specialists emerged, and through trade, so did wealth. Wealth and position combined to form a new but essential element in the world of art, the patron. The needs and tastes of the patron have exercised more influence on the evolution of art than any other single factor. Technological improvements have determined the course of art reproduction and distribution, but have had basically little impact on the art itself.

Artists do not draw any more skillfully today than did their ancestors. But, the patrons have changed. When the church was all powerful, art was overwhelmingly religious in character. Today, few are the artists who could survive painting only Madonnas. Naturalists have never been a major factor among patrons, and so animal art has evolved within the context of other kinds of art.

This evolution has followed two paths: violence and gentleness. In both cases the motivating force has been the philosophy summed up in Genesis in which God instructed man 'to subdue' the earth, and 'have dominion over the fish of the sea, and over the fowl of the air, and over every living thing that moveth upon the earth.'

Man had to subdue, and man had dominion. This attitude permeated animal art for centuries. The Babylonians had Gilgamesh whom the Jews resurrected as Samson, who slew the lion with the jawbone of an ass. The Greeks and Romans had Hercules whose twelve labours largely revolved around overcoming animal foes. All this provided heroic material for animals in art. One of the earliest animal sculptures, dating from the 4th millennium B.C., shows Gilgamesh crushing a lion with his left hand, heroically and stoically unmoved by the fact that the claws of the expiring beast are embedded in his groin. Hercules slaying everything in sight also figured prominently in Greek and Roman sculpture and painting.

In later years, patrons saw themselves as supermen; Egyptian pharaohs had themselves immortalized in tomb paintings depicting hunts whose outcome, at least as far as the lion was concerned, was never in doubt. The violent end of animals at the hand of man is splattered across endless canvasses from the Italian Renaissance, when noblemen had their hunting scenes painted under such religious guises as *The Adoration of the Magi* and *The Flight to Egypt*. Violence had the blessing of Genesis. Today, hunting scenes still command a great following, and many are the duck and game paintings conceived through the sights of a gun.

Paralleling this violence, however, was man's compassion and appreciation for animals. The second part of Genesis emerges here: man has dominion. Overwhelmingly, animals were depicted serving or being enjoyed by man. Egyptian cats, sacred ibis of wood and gold, faience falcons and hippopotomuses with papyrus painted on their hips – animals were revered in the ancient kingdoms of the Nile. Even the written language was replete with beautifully rendered, if stylized, animals. Ibis, bulls, chicks, snakes, vultures, eagles and lions are but a few of the hieroglyphs. Never has there been an artistic tradition more thoroughly mixed with animals.

While Hercules was slaying, the early 6th century B.C. artist, Exekias, was creating a flat drinking cup in whose shallow bowl Dionysus sails forever in the company of seven beautiful dolphins. A century later a sublime rooster is held aloft by Ganymede on a large mixing bowl. As the main medium of artistic expression, tens of thousands of pieces of pottery contained nonviolent animals in Greek art. On a grander scale, no equestrian statue surpassed the perfection

of the heads of the two horses, representing the sun and the moon, which extended beyond the corners of the pediment of the Parthenon of 438-431 B.C. And throughout the Age of Pericles, Athena's owl blinked wisely from the city's coinage.

The various artistic traditions of the ancient world obeyed the classical adage that all roads led to Rome, for it was in Roman art that the full flowering of wildlife was realized. Innumerable hunting scenes attest the concern with animal combat in the colosseums of the empire. But, animals were often shown in a gentle way that would not be matched for another two thousand years. Whole walls of sophisticated houses were decorated with fields, fruits, flowers, games, fish and birds, all accurately portrayed in the most artistic manner. Animals were even depicted for their own sake quite independently from man. Then in A.D. 79 Vesuvius blew and buried Pompeii and Herculaneum under a thick layer of volcanic ash. Had Rome not fallen, there is no way of telling what the future course of animal art would have been. As it was, it took the western world almost two thousand years to catch up to Pompeii.

All art suffered during the Dark Ages. By the 12th century, animals had become stylized absurdities. It was as if nothing had come before. Significantly, no new book on natural history had been written to replace the *Historia Naturalis* of Pliny, who had

died in the eruption of Vesuvius that buried Pompeii. No one seemed to question the existence of Pliny's whales hundreds of feet long, three feet wide, and which 'took up in length as much as foure acres or arpens of land.' Nor did anyone seem to care that Pliny had drawn heavily on Aristotle and even earlier sources.

Artists, however, could not help but see a different world. The crushing veil of a millennium and a half was finally lifted with the rise of the secular city-state and the profound earthliness of the Church. New markets for art were opened, fuelled by the egos, tastes and pocketbooks of the power brokers of the Renaissance. From a modern viewpoint it is here in the earliest years of the 14th century that the threads of our animal art traditions begin to weave their tapestry.

In the 1300s painting replaced mosaics as the main medium of expression. Stiffness gave way to freedom of line, and the range of subjects expanded greatly. Nature, in part or in whole, played an increasing role. Countless angels hovered on aerodynamically ridiculous wings whose feathers had become mathematical exercises in overlapping patterns of colour. Wings were too spectacular to be wasted on mere birds. But where would Saint Francis of Assisi have been without birds? Artists began paying attention to specific species. A panel of *Christ in the Garden of Olives* in Prague circa 1350 shows a bullfinch, a goldfinch and a hoopoe, complete with Peterson-style field marks. Admittedly these birds had religious significance, but without accuracy the symbolism could not have been identified.

At the beginning of the 15th century we find attention being paid to wildflowers for the first time. Circa 1420 the Master of the Middle Rhine painted a *Garden in Paradise* carpeted with flawless lily-of-the-valley, iris, strawberries in fruit and flower, calla lilies and climbing roses. But realism did not progress uninterruptedly. Even someone as enormously talented as Sandro Botticelli (1445-1510) regressed. The delicate flowers in his *Primavera* gave way to totally abstract, insignificant trees in paintings he did after falling under the influence of Savanarola's ravings.

Leonardo da Vinci was probably born in 1452, Michelangelo in 1475, and Raphael in 1483. Apart from some monumental equestrian statuary (and a remarkable turtle on a salt cellar by Benvenuto Cellini), animal art during their era was disappointing. For them, the human body was supreme, and their animals were always subordinated. Lambs looked lovingly at Holy families, Madonnas held goldfinches, and vapid aristocratic ladies petted their ermines.

Leonardo sketched scores of anatomical studies of cats, dogs, cows and even dragonflies. His studies of horses included every layer of muscle and the skeleton itself. Only George Stubbs, three centuries later, would devote as much investigation to animal anatomy. Botanically, Leonardo made these studies to fix in his mind the differences in branching patterns of elms and elders, and he analysed how light and shade played on trees and plants. This detailed knowledge was not translated into any significant work of animal art. The sketches remained buried.

It was different with Albrecht Dürer, the great painter of the Northern Renaissance, who lovingly included animals and plants in his woodcuts, portraits and landscapes. His young owl, young hare, two squirrels and a clump of turf are still considered among the most outstanding ever produced.

In the Holy Roman Empire, Titian, Velásquez, Tintoretto and other great artists included animals in their art, but they and their contemporaries felt that the study of animal anatomy was beneath them, and some even boasted of having no knowledge whatsoever of the animal world. Their horses, as animal art, were an embarrassment. By 1600, however, Caravaggio was creating the most beautiful horses ever painted by a non-wildlife artist. Unfortunately, they were not only subordinated to man, they were also subordinated to Carravaggio's own art. Their well-groomed flanks and wonderful muscles served primarily as surfaces on which light and shadow could play. Frequently he showed only a portion of the body with the head fading into the darkened background.

Then Peter Paul Rubens (1577-1640) erupted voluptuously onto the scene with great rounded horses contorting amid fat, pink, dimpled ladies. The distortions of Rubens' animals can almost be overlooked because of the dramatic and compositional roles they play in the overall picture. However, his paintings would not meet the high criteria demanded of wildlife painters today.

In contrast are the life-size bulls and cows by Dutchman Paulus Potter (1625-1654). His large landscape in which are set two small but wonderfully drawn stags silhouetted against the sky would certainly stand up to today's standards. Below the brow of the small hill on which they stand a wild boar snuffles through the grass. There is no sign of man; wildlife art is flirting with respectability in its own right.

But not quite. The finest bird portrait of the period – one of the greatest of all times – was a small – 13 1/4 x 9 inch – European Goldfinch done by Carel Fabritius, the disciple of Rembrandt and the master of Vermeer.

Study of Great Horned Owl and Jackrabbit

It was painted in the year of his death, 1654. A simple bird, tethered by a fine link chain to a wooden perch against a plain wall, the Goldfinch is masterfully painted. The featheration and colour are remarkable for the impressionism, not their finicky detail. It was not considered at the time to be a masterpiece, or even a serious painting. It was intended as a panel for a cupboard door.

In 1741, the great French painter Jean-Baptiste Chardin painted a still life of a dead hare, suspended by a foot, with the body appropriately limp and the fur matted and lank. The French term for still life, *nature morte*, was never more appropriate. This matted fur and limp body required great drawing skill, but an even greater skill in observation. Two hundred and forty years later, George McLean painted the matted fur and lifeless body of a hare battered by a Great Horned Owl. Even the back foot, just visible along the rock, is turned the wrong way, broken by the owl's death grasp.

The horse has played a preponderant role in animal art from antiquity. Two Frenchmen, Théodore Géricault (1791-1824) and Eugène Delacroix (1798-1863) carried their love of equestrian subjects to an exaggerated degree. Nevertheless, their overstatements made animals in art wildly popular during the early 19th century. Géricault considered the horse the incarnation of the lifeforce, and his gigantic semi-tamed stallions were more dramatic in

stance, muscle and movement than anything ever seen in nature. Delacroix's horses were also romanticized, as were the other animals in his epic paintings. He painted a tiger hunt in which a wounded cat is attached to the flank of a terrified horse while the rider looks on in trepidation. The scene is filled with drama; the animals are an absurdity, which is unfortunate, because no one could sketch lions, for instance, more brilliantly than Delacroix. Had Delacroix and Géricault had the field to themselves, animal art would have regressed to a worship not of nature but of an artist's mannerisms. Fortunately, there were powerful forces at work elsewhere. This was the great age of landscape painting, and its importance for animal art is fundamental. Without skillful handling of the setting, the animal artist rapidly reverts to scientific draughtsmanship or mere illustration.

During the heyday of England's astonishingly talented watercolourists there were endless examples of animals in art. Flocks by the thousands dotted light-bathed fields; cows by the hundreds chewed their cud under towering trees or stood placidly ankle deep in gentle rivers. There is a certain sameness about these animals, particularly in the paintings of such fine artists as George Fennel Robson, George Barret Jr. and James Ward. The explanation is that all of them were done by the same person, Robert Hills. It is important to study Hills because his work is, in a way, the perfect antithesis to McLean's art. Hills is the ultimate expression of animals *in* art.

Hills was born in 1769 and died in 1844, living during the height of popularity for watercolours and landscapes. A founder and first Secretary of the Old Water-Colour Society in 1804, he was a very talented watercolourist in his own right, but was best known as an animal painter for other people's work. Between 1806 and 1816 he published one of the most unusual books on natural history ever produced. The title of the seven folio volume opus is as self-explanatory as it is revealing: *Etchings of Quadrupeds, Comprising Rudiments of Drawing, and Numerous Series of Groups for the Embellishment of Landscape Scenery*. There was no text and no scientific classification. The thousands of original engravings were expressly intended to be copied by others who needed groups for artistic placement in landscapes. In every conceivable pose, there were groups of cows, horses, roebuck, dogs, goats, asses and mules. There were also detailed studies of horns, hooves and hindquarters which clearly demonstrated Hills' acute powers of observation and painstaking study.

In 1771, John Robert Cozens, another great watercolourist and teacher, had anticipated Hills in another key element of landscape art when he published *The Shape, Skeleton and Foliage of Thirty-Two Species of Trees for the Use of Paintings and Drawings*.

The animals of Hills and the trees of Cozens are very important not for their accuracy, but rather for what they represent. They were merely adjuncts to landscape. What was important was that the landscape be pleasing, and pleasing was defined as accurate. The 19th century landscape painting had its genesis in draughtsmanship for military reconnaissance, in which it was essential for the artist to master placement and perspective. Getting in all the facts was more important than aesthetics.

To this austere base, John Constable (1776-1837) added a realization of the importance of the sky, and by extension, of light and clouds upon which so much of the mood of a landscape depends. Constable's innovations had an immense impact on animal art. Mixing a real landscape, bathed in a real atmosphere, with an obviously artificial group of animals caused a tension that could not last. Within a few years of Hills' folios, John Thomas Smith (1768-1833), an artist friend of Constable, wrote: 'Do not set about inventing figures for a landscape taken from nature, for you cannot remain an hour in any spot, however solitary, without the appearance of some living thing that will, in all probability, accord better with the scene and time of day than will any invention of your own.' It was no longer acceptable to use animals as props to satisfy the current compositional canons of taste.

The final breakthrough in wildlife art came in 1827 when John James Audubon appeared out of nowhere to exhibit his *Birds of America*. The impact of Audubon on the subsequent course of animal art cannot be overstated. Audubon's intent was to publish a monumental book in which all American species would be portrayed life-size and in their proper ecological setting. In a single flash wildlife art catapulted to the forefront of all art. European art critics were thrown into turmoil. Audubon was lionized, made a member of every learned society, courted by crowned heads, and generally captivated Europe. How could this phenomenon be explained in a France where artists were still posturing with exaggerated horses (Delacroix was still alive, and Géricault had died three years previously), and where a love affair with things Egyptian was still torrid? Landscape was, however, artistically acceptable. Only in this context can we understand the astonishing review of the Edinburgh exhibition, written by Philatère Chasles for *Le Monde*: 'Imagine! A landscape wholly American, trees, flowers, grasses, even the tints of the sky and waters, quickened with a life that is real, peculiar, trans-Atlantic... It is a real and palpable vision of the New World, with its atmospheres, its imposing vegetation.' All this for an exhibition of bird art! Audubon had painted not just the reality of birds, but of birds within a landscape or floral setting which was now secondary. The animals had become dominant, and yet the results were incontestably great art.

The fundamental strength of Audubon's paintings is clearly labelled at the bottom left hand corner of his plates: 'Drawn from Nature.' Audubon travelled tens of thousands of miles through the wilderness of North America compiling an unmatched store of firsthand field experience. He knew more about the animals and their environment than all the previous American naturalists combined. His perception was so astonishing that he saw what no one else had been able to record, or, in some cases, what no one else was willing to believe until photography, time and again, proved him right.

His fame today rests mainly on his bird paintings, and too few people realize that he was also one of the greatest mammal painters of all time. In his lesser known *Viviparous Quadrupeds of North America* his handling of the textures of various types of fur, the vivacity he imparted to the eyes, the tension in the muscles, and the innate ability to create the artistically superlative and ecologically accurate settings set standards that exceed the ability of most animal artists today.

By the 1840s the vicissitudes of Audubon's life had taken their toll. Halfway through the *Quadrupeds* he turned his brushes over to his technically talented son, John Woodhouse Audubon, who completed at least 71 of the paintings. Audubon by this time had raised the level of animal art to such heights that numerous extraordinarily talented artists, who had, as it were, been waiting in the wings, emerged to expand wildlife painting to the farthest corners of the earth. As an 18-year-old, Edward Lear published a monograph on the parrot family that immediately ranked him among the greatest ornithological draughtsmen of all time. One criticism can be laid against him – incredibly, he was too accurate. He transcribed every feather so perfectly that the pattern of the individual bird may not have been typical of the species as a whole.

John Gould, the great bird book impressario for whom Lear did many hand-coloured lithographs, wrote in the preface to the folio *The Birds of Europe*: 'His (Lear's) abilities as an artist are so generally acknowledged that any comments of my own are unnecessary.' A few might have helped. Even within his own lifetime other artists felt free to plagiarize Lear's great compositions, and as recently as 1979 a Lear painting was ascribed to John Gould in what purported to be a serious work on ornithological art. In 1837 deteriorating health forced Lear to move to Italy where he soon styled himself a landscape painter.

The best of Gould's artists was Joseph Wolf, a man of such towering genius that Sir Edwin Landseer called him 'without exception the best all-round animal painter that ever lived.' In his youth he haunted and hunted the woods of his native Germany with an old forester. He knew the habits and peculiarities of his subjects from vast field experience, heightened by an eyesight which was legendary even during his own lifetime. In later years he asked that his favourite truth be inscribed on the title page of his biography: 'We see distinctly only what we know thoroughly.'

He was obsessed with scientific accuracy, completing scores of full-size drawings of the tarsus and foot, giving the exact shape and position of the scales and the scutellae. Each bird was frequently sketched two or three times in virtual architectural or engineering drawings. He was an artist who was resolutely determined not to become a mere scientific draughtsman and refused to succumb to the stiff profiles demanded by the orthodoxy of scientific illustration. He was pleased when a leading zoologist complained that 'Wolf just can't draw birds the way we want them.'

Wolf was at home with virtually every animal. He understood how fur breaks and feathers overlap. He could have a green boa sagging under its own weight from the branch of a tropical tree, or have hippos truly wallowing. A dozing lynx or a fenec fox with alert ears displayed his understanding of the character of the animals. Through Wolf, science and art were at last reconciled.

For the detailed drawings of Daniel Elliott's great monograph on *Pheasants* (1870-1872), Wolf turned the work over to John Keulemans, who was to tower over the rest of the animal art world for another three decades, and of whom Wolf admiringly said, 'That young man really observes his birds.' But Keulemans was emphatically Wolf's protégé. As numerous (over 2000 finished paintings) and as outstanding as the plates were, Keulemans represents the final extension of Joseph Wolf. Even more, Keulemans was the final expositor of the 19th century tradition in which the bird or animal totally dominated the compositions in lifelike but in more or less static and decorative poses. A new age was dawning. In Lord Lilford's *Coloured Figures of Birds of the British Islands* (1885-1897), Keulemans contributed 61 of the more than 300 plates. Two hundred and forty were by an extraordinary newcomer, Archibald Thorburn, who at age 23 showed in this first commission that he had far surpassed Wolf, Keulemans and other talented contemporaries. He represented a major evolutionary step. He conceived of his work as an artist first, as a lover of nature second and he thought in terms of a total composition rather than of a bird with a composition around it.

The hallmark of Thorburn's work was a remarkable sense of depth. He would build up his pictures in different planes starting literally and figuratively at the viewer's feet. The various poses and elements lead the viewer bodily into the painting. This feeling of depth was heightened by Thorburn's unprecedented grasp of light – direct, reflected or diffused. Atmosphere, as with Constable, had become an integral part of the composition. Sunlight would bounce up off wet sand and highlight the belly of a gull where previous artists had painted shadows. The use of light created an enveloping atmosphere that extended beyond the confines of the canvas and which wrapped the viewer in a shared environment. Whether they were paintings of birds, seals, whales, mice or rabbits in the snow, his art added a sense of participation. Something new was added to wildlife art: intimacy. Before Thorburn, absolutely nothing like this had been attempted. Animal painting as art in the academic sense had come of age, and become ageless. In 1972, the *London Observer* published a miniature bird book with 201 plates. They were, of course, reproductions of what Thorburn had done for Lilford three-quarters of a century earlier.

And then there appeared the two European painters who are the artistic ancestors of McLean, and who developed wildlife art in a way never achieved by Thornburn, Keulemans, Wolf and Audubon. These two were Bruno Liljefors of Sweden, and Léo-Paul Robert of Switzerland. They carried animal art a quantum leap beyond anything that had come before, but without the cumulative tradition they – like McLean – could never have just happened. More than any other North American artist, McLean echoes, builds on and embellishes the legacy of these two consummate masters.

Liljefors was born in rural Uppsala in 1860, and spent his formative years in his father's gunpowder shop listening to the local farmers and hunters sharing their knowledge of the forests and fields and their inhabitants. His love of nature became all consuming, and he honed his powers of observation during endless days out of doors. His eyesight, like Wolf's, was extraordinary; a cartoonist friend described him as 'simply one concentrated eye.' Once, when a flock of gulls flew by, Liljefors looked up and said one bird had a damaged foot. Later, when the bird landed, an observer saw one limping. As important as his eyesight was his prodigious memory.

He could sketch the detail and mood of species new to him hours after having seen them. He studied in Germany, but soon tired of the dark palette of his teacher. He discovered Japanese prints and was profoundly struck by the way in which the artists never imposed themselves on the scene through mannerisms. The subject reigned supreme.

Liljefors was in love with nature. 'Organic life,' he said, 'especially animal, is the apex of creation, and movement is the highest expression of natural life.' He added, 'Opposing forces permeate all life. That is the foundation of beauty.' This appreciation of energy echoes poet William Blake's credo that 'Energy is eternal delight; exuberance is beauty.' By this definition, Liljefors' paintings are beautiful. Many artists today, however, lie closer to Edmund Burke's definition of beauty found in his *Philosophical Enquiry into the Origins of our Ideas of the Sublime and Beautiful*, which appeared in 1757. Burke considered smoothness as the most essential ingredient in beauty. Roughness, on the other hand, formed the fundamental difference between beauty and the picturesque. To lovers of bucolic landscapes, and to a whole host of draughtsmen today, Liljefors is rough, and therefore not beautiful. Minor artists cannot begin to understand, let alone emulate, the overpowering beauty that bursts from Liljefors' bold brushwork and subdued range of colours. Where Liljefors had understanding and technique, lesser painters substitute mannerisms and formulae.

Liljefors understood that too much smoothness produced blandness, and that some roughness was necessary to inject a note of reality but not necessarily realism in the detailed sense.

He felt absolutely no need to paint every feather or piece of fur. Nor was it essential for every blade of grass or every leaf to be drawn down to the last vein, or every flower to the last petal. This in no way indicated laziness, a lack of knowledge, or a lack of talent. On the contrary, he worked assiduously from his earliest years to understand and to reproduce with total fidelity the physical and mechanical aspects of his subjects. Liljefors could paint accurately without giving the impression that detail had become a preoccupation. He had seen the Impressionist paintings in Paris at the Salon of 1883, and he immediately recognized that he must paint light to achieve form. He would never be a linear painter.

Above all, Liljefors' paintings were a celebration of movement. Eiders whirr over curling waves, wingtips blurred; moose trot over autumnal tundra, hooves and legs blending with the land and vegetation; a rabbit pauses for a moment against snow painted from the same brushfuls of colour, the wetness of early spring seeping up through the footprints that lead the viewer's eye to the subject just before it darts away. Nothing is static. Movement is measured and assured, never a nervous flurry. The birds and mammals are so logically and naturally balanced that no position, however contorted, becomes ugly. This ease of handling movement flowed from his complete trust in his own ability.

His compositions astound. Too many artists represent their subjects in what are so obviously poses, rather than trying to capture what nature happens to present. A Curlew will land in a field exactly in the spot where it is least likely to be seen. To downplay the obvious, Liljefors places the bird off centre, in the lower left quadrant facing out of the picture. All the cute formulae of the art schools is discarded in favour of truth. In other canvasses, the birds are so well camouflaged by their concealing colouration that they can be seen easily only through their reflections in a small pool. His paintings are witnesses of an unexpected event in which neither the artist nor the viewer intrudes. We may have actually witnessed a comparable scene, but what we grasped and remembered only subconsciously, Liljefors has absorbed and recreated so that it hits us like a blow and we are strongly moved by it.

No one described the emotional impact of Liljefors' paintings better than his biographer, K.E. Russow, who had once sat by the shore of the Baltic watching thousands of ducks whirring away westwards and who 'remained there until dark, enthralled by the spectacle and quietly pondering. Millions of warmblooded creatures were migrating, as they had done for thousands upon thousands of years every autumn. It seemed like the pulse of Eternity. Ten years later... I saw a picture representing a flight of Eider duck above a large, green wave. I do not know how long I remained before that painting; I passed and repassed it several times. I was again in the grip of the same perception of Eternity that I had experienced that night by the storm-swept shore. The name of Bruno Liljefors that day indelibly stamped itself on my memory.'

The pulse of Eternity: the same feeling flows from the paintings of the other great European influence on McLean's work. Léo-Paul Robert's ecological bird paintings, which he started producing in 1869 when he was only 18-years-old, through his death in 1923, are perhaps the finest bird portraits ever before modern times. Yet, outside his native Switzerland, Robert has remained basically unknown. Even within Switzerland he is best remembered as a classical artist, trained in landscape, or more accurately mountain, field and forest scapes. He imbued his vast canvasses and murals with a luminosity born of the clear Alpine air. The light has to be seen to be believed.

His wildlife career started in earnest when he created a series of plates, for use in Swiss schools to familiarize children with small birds. The paintings promptly won a Silver

Medal at the Universal Exposition of 1878 in Paris. (It is an irony that Liljefors won the Gold Medal at Munich in 1892 for his *Capercalzie Hunter*, in which no bird can actually be seen. The viewer looks over the shoulder of a hunter who is carefully scanning a darkling forest for the largest member of the grouse family. Fickle art critics had decided that animal art was no longer in vogue; Liljefors and all of Sweden knew better.) As the school plates were exclusively for Swiss consumption, arrangements were made to reproduce them in three sumptuously ornate volumes published in Paris in 1879. The publisher, M.D. Lebet, sensed that some of the brilliance and subtlety of the originals would be lost through reproduction. He expressed the wish that 'whether chromolithographed or engraved, the compositions of Monsieur Robert would clearly express the difference that by necessity must exist between art which draws its inspiration from living nature and that which copies *la nature morte*.' (The French term for still life clearly implies death, and well describes the work of painters who have faithfully copied every mistake of the taxidermist at the local museum.) With all their

inadequacies, the reproductions of the plates were awarded a Gold Medal by the French Minister of Agriculture in 1884, and La Grande Medaille d'Or of the International Ornithological Congress of Vienna that same year. The originals would not be reproduced again until 1934 in a posthumous edition with the finest Swiss colour printing. A page from this book introduced North Americans to Robert at the Royal Ontario Museum's *Animals in Art* exhibition. George McLean was among those overwhelmed by the display.

The excellence of Robert's settings could be expected from his training. His handling of small flowers, trees, leaves and branches is a marvel. A contemporary critic described his meadows as being 'enamelled with flowers, where a thousand petals sparkle in the sun. But in reality, this exquisite detail was handled with the broadest and simplest approach.' The total impact was so convincing that the viewer tended not to notice that the detail was, in fact, totally impressionistic. Robert's meadow setting for his whinchat, van Gogh's field of poppies, and the wildflowers for McLean's masterpiece *Eastern Bluebirds and Cornflowers* all spring from the same ethos. In Robert's painting of the crested tits an adult feeds a family of young sitting on a pine branch. The backdrop is a tapestry of interwoven boughs that seem to sigh in the wind. The details are totally lacking, but a sense of space, mass, even organic relationship, is achieved with a few brushstrokes and an exquisitely limited palette. There is an uncanny similarity between Robert's treatment of the forest and that of McLean's painting of the owl

swooping on the squirrel. Robert seldom attempted to portray actual movement; the alertness of his birds underlined their *potential* for movement. With the incredible activity of the owl and the squirrel, McLean's painting would not have flowed from Robert's brushes. His background, however, could have.

To an astonishing degree, what can be said about Robert and Liljefors can also be said about McLean. The traditions of so many artists and so many centuries come together in a flawless amalgam. Their birds and mammals are totally alive. McLean can approach foreshortening with such ease that the complexities of perspective never interfere with the attitudes in which the birds are shown. Lesser artists perhaps would have used foreshortening to emphasize, to shock, or even to show off their mastery of the mathematical formulae. They would not understand that mathematically perfect perspective without a sense of art becomes the antithesis of art. Free of all such considerations, McLean can create a naturalness that has not been surpassed and only seldom equalled.

It is the same with the composition of their paintings. A portion of rock outcropping or a cliff can extend well beyond the field of vision when the eye is concentrating on the bird, but the brain automatically and instantaneously fills in the parts that are missing. In the paintings of all three, rocks,

blades of grass, flowers, branches and frequently the birds and mammals extend beyond what is seen to exist into what is known to exist. The physical borders of the pictures, therefore, cease to impose any artistic limits. With this endless freedom, their paintings could be square, rectangular, horizontal or vertical and of any size without compromising the artistry. This approach differs fundamentally from that of an artist who starts with a blank space and feels obliged to fill it, or who conceives of a layout within the confines of a white border.

With McLean, as with Robert and Liljefors, it is as if the viewer were looking out through a window. The birds seem unaware that a moment in their lives is being shared by an unseen observer. Nothing seems posed. As they go about their appointed tasks, even the smallest passerines take on an almost heroic quality. The hare in winter is no less worthy of artistic genius than the largest moose. All the creatures are the successful products of eons of evolution.

Black-crowned Night Heron

THE ART

'Look at that!' George exclaimed, as two swallows careened by. What I saw and what he saw were two different things. In his mind the impression was broken down into its component parts of form, movement, colour and environment. I only saw two careening swallows. Combined with other past experiences, McLean's impression would be translated onto paper, the elements refined, and a major painting would some-day appear.

We went to his studio to discuss the act of creating. The studio itself set the stage, for it was here that owl and squirrel were contending in the unfinished painting. Strewn about on shelves, floor, couches, tables and mantel were endless mines of inspiration, stimulation and reference. There were books and portfolios of paintings by Liljefors, Andrew Wyeth, photographic essays and zoological treatises on African game and North American mammals. Old ammunition ads by Terry Shortt vied for space with back issues of *Audubon* and *National Geographic*. Trays of slides teetered on the brink of disaster. Paul Bransom's sketches and old articles, incomplete sets of Brooke-Bond bird cards from his youth, and sketch pads

and notes from Bob Kuhn lay in disarray. Fox, wolf, lynx and mountain lion pelts hung from pegs or over chair backs. A raccoon's tail spilled from a shelf near a deer head (from Paul Bransom's studio). Branches and twigs from a hemlock were close at hand to the easel; they would come to life again under the owl's outstretched talons. There was a fungus from a yellow birch root, essential for accuracy in another painting also underway. The floor was carpeted with photostats of sketches that had been blown up to the size they would ultimately be as finished paintings.

Only a truly ordered mind could sort out the myriad facets of this wonderful clutter of past, present and future. McLean does not paint in a vacuum.

I questioned what function some of the curled photos served. 'I'll extract the essence from a given photo,' he explained, 'but it will be out of view for the rest of the time. I

let the texture of the paint do things a photo simply is incapable of achieving.

'And,' he added thoughtfully, 'it doesn't really matter how a painting is done, providing it's done well. It starts with drawing.'

The great French artist, Degas, once said: 'Drawing is not a matter of shape. It is the way shapes are seen.' 'Look at that!' George had said. How would he see the shapes? How would he see the form?

A distinction can be made between a linear painter and a painter of light. At opposite ends of the spectrum, the differences are obvious. Audubon and Wolf and most 19th century animal painters were linear. They went after their outlines with a vengeance and basically coloured them in. The edges tended to be sharply defined and there was usually an emphasis on precise detail. Moving towards the centre, Lear, with his training as a watercolourist and landscapist, softened the outlines, while Thorburn added the role of light. At the other end of the spectrum we find Liljefors and Robert who understood that detail could be downplayed if the values were accurate.

Crouched Lynx

Most animal painters have, for whatever reason, opted to align their art nearer the linear end of the artistic spectrum. Fewer paint light. Perhaps the qualified painter of light has a more difficult job cut out for him, for his excellence must be founded as much on specific knowledge as on abstract principles. There is a need to see things in terms of abstractions, not just in terms of surface reality. Conceptually, if the artist wants to capture the essence he must start with an abstraction and build up layers of reality. He also has to know when to quit, because too much reality runs the risk of masking, distorting or obliterating.

It is certainly possible to draw a fish by starting with an individual scale, multiplying it outward until a body emerges. Instinctively, we know that this is the wrong approach. The essence of a fish is not the scale multiplied by other scales any more than the essence of the bird is a multiplication of feathers.

At the other extreme, there are artists whose emphasis on form at the expense or exclusion of detail result in a painting whose message and context are incomprehensible. In animal art this can become an artistic affectation of the worst kind. In the process of leaving things out the artist did not know when to quit, and suddenly there was nothing left.

The concepts are hard to convey. McLean tends to paint light rather than line. He emphasizes abstract form and gives the impression of detail. In the process, he captures that most elusive of elements, the

Leopard

essence. He paints the animals the way they are, not the way a superficial observer thinks they ought to look. His portrait *Young Lioness* is a classic example. The skin, as

she stands there, is several sizes too big. But this is exactly what a young lioness looks like. There is nothing of the sleek power that

25

we associate with the huntress. The potential is there, but it has not yet been realized. The folds of skin will become taut when she is running, as her power stretches her form.

McLean is fascinated with the feline form. It is to him what the horse was to Géricault and Delacroix. Liljefors had his pet cat, Jeppe; McLean had Charlie, a grey and white delight that stealthily walked the timbers by an old barn in search of an unseen mouse. And it was Charlie stalking through a meadow for whatever chance might bring. The essence of being a cat has seldom been rendered so wonderfully as in McLean's paintings of Charlie. Within his own size frame, Charlie is every bit as heroic as the cougar slung across the branches of a tree, dozing the sleep of a cat, ready at a moment's notice to defend or attack. The giant paws combine awesome power with the sense of affection that only cat lovers understand. The perch is not designed for a cat that size, and only the counterforce of the tail allows the beast to defy gravity. The tail does not simply hang down. It is true muscle and bone, adding a tension which forces the viewer subconsciously to react to the latent strength of the largest North American cat.

Cats are consummate hunters, and their very nature implies violence. McLean has not feared to portray this side of their existence. For some strange reason, artists have shied away from depicting raw meat in their

Cougar Reclining

canvasses. The examples of meat paintings are extremely few and far between. Circa 2450 B.C. the Tomb of Ptahinuk in the Nile Valley had a fresco showing a flayed ox. His pink entrails showed through the incision in his stomach. Enter the patron. Ptahinuk was identified as the Superintendent of Slaughterhouses! Almost four thousand years later Rembrandt portrayed another flayed ox, carcass spread, ribs and red meat there for the slicing. In 1978 McLean painted a crouching tiger, semi-snarling to ward off an unseen intruder while he feasts on a bleeding haunch he has just ripped off the dead water buffalo which lies oozing blood in the background of tall grasses. But McLean's violence is not man induced. It is nature's plan, and its portrayal implies no moralizing or sermon. Anthropomorphism has absolutely no place in good animal art. The tiger has killed because that is his role. There is no aggressor, and no innocent victim.

Capturing the essence of a bird is almost a greater challenge because there is less with which to work. The feathers mask the muscle and bone, and the eyes in their large orbits do not give the artist the same freedom of expression. The essence is manifest through pose, carriage and form. All these, however, demand a rendering of feathers, the one thing that all birds have in common. Few people – and, it would seem, few artists – truly understand the physical properties of the different types of feathers. McLean does. The feathers of an owl are soft and contoured. The flight feathers are fringed to baffle all noise, for owls are ghosts you do not hear. Yet, when an eagle or large hawk folds its wings in a steep dive, the feathers rattle like cardboard. The tail feathers of a woodpecker are as stiff and resilient as a piece of whalebone. Egret plumes react to the wind and to their own weight in a manner that bears no relation to the erectile crest of a cardinal. And, as we see in McLean's powerful portrait of the *Bald Eagle* on the branch of the white pine, the tail feathers have a totally different texture from the contour feathers or the hackles skirting the neck. In the painting *Ruffed Grouse Displaying* the rigidity of the fanned tail, emphasized by the straight-on foreshortening, could not be more unlike the wispy feathers of the rump. On the smaller birds, such as blue jays and bluebirds, the body feathers split and dissolve almost into hairs so that their outline is completely lost. Any artist who paints them in is pandering to the demand of detail for detail's sake, not for the sake of art or accuracy.

McLean's paintings reflect Liljefors' statement that 'movement is the highest expression of natural life.' Often this involves flight. For an artist, it requires more than just the extension of wings to achieve a convincing sense of flying. The Italian Renaissance produced masterpieces (Piero di Cosimo, 1462-1521, *The Forest Fire*) which make us wince at the sight of feathered bombs being hurled by an unseen hand through the air. These birds obviously have absolutely no control over their own destiny. Their flight path follows the predetermined parabola of a football.

Equally distressing is the habit of many of today's artists who freeze the wingtips in linear focus despite the inability of the human eye to define the outlines of feathers that are beating several times per second. Painting a wing in flight with clear detail is a denial of the laws of aerodynamics and optics. Visually, the wing tips should be out of focus if the sense of flight is to be achieved. The starlings escaping from the Red-tailed Hawk and the male bluebird in the summer meadow depicted by McLean offer prime examples.

The evolutionary process has created different ways of flying, each suited to the particular niche filled by a species. A trained bird watcher can identify most birds, at least at the family level, by their flight. At even moderate distances, feather patterns and colour are not significant in identification, especially when the bird is seen against the sky, which makes virtually every bird look dark. It is all the more important, therefore, to depict the flight pattern peculiar to a species, and for this the positioning of the wings is crucial. The shoulder-high stroking of McLean's blue jay among the trilliums contrasts with the high-winged silence of his Short-eared Owl braking in mid air as he turns towards the lookout post.

There are other aspects of flying in McLean's paintings. A hawk will always aim slightly below the bird he is attacking, whereas an owl will aim above the fleeing rabbit or squirrel. The broad belly of a duck flattens into an airfoil during landing. Less easy to define and infinitely more difficult to capture is what can be called the motive of flight. The soaring of a vulture above the resting lioness is fundamentally different from the explosive flight of the starlings scattering under the attack of the Red-tailed Hawk. (Incidentally, the starlings in McLean's paintings are as good as free. Unless the hawk can get them in tall grass, he will not have a chance.) The complete lack of concern of a hawk for the winds buffeting the tree tops bears scant relation to the methodical wing beats of a migrating robin. These are all different types of flight.

But birds also fly differently depending on what they are doing. An Osprey lifts laboriously off the water with a fish in his talons; the entire axis of the body relative to the angle of the neck is very different from the same relationships when the bird is soaring or preparing to land. A hawk rising on unseen thermals positions his wings differently than when stooping on his prey. Only a trained field observer can tell at a glance whether the artist has portrayed flight in a manner appropriate to the bird and to the act in which the bird is depicted.

Just as a sense of buoyancy in air must be created, so too there must be a convincing sense of birds floating in water. This requires an ability to draw water, especially reflected patterns on the surface under the reflective and refractive influence of waves, and above all it requires a knowledge of the avian Plimsoll line. The loon always looks as if it were about to sink, ducks do not. Phalaropes, Mergansers, gulls and Canada geese have different centres of gravity, and therefore float higher or lower in the water with their fulcrum forwards or backwards.

McLean's family of Canada geese shows how intimately he knows his subject. The water line is exactly where it should be. The adults float confidently, the male alert for predators, the female solicitous for her goslings. The family is weaving its way through a natural channel in the reeds, leading the viewer into the picture with them. Motion is emphasized by the serpentine route which can only be traced in a stately rather than frantic pace. Special attention has been paid to the wave patterns and the light on the water beyond the reeds.

Both pattern and waves are changed by the interference of the plants, further heightening the sense of movement through the subtle contrasts.

For mammals, the question of motion is translated from wings to feet, from feathers to fur. The feeling of motion is brilliantly portrayed in McLean's painting of the Golden Lab chasing the cottontail. He has captured a split second; one more bound and both will have disappeared. The dog is totally absorbed in concentration on the fleeing rabbit, which is equally intent on escape. Between the two there is an invisible line which inexorably draws the focus of the viewer's attention to a blank section of the composition. The brain rejects this, and the eye is forced to search again for a resting point that simply is not there. The very involvement of the viewer imparts a sense of motion. There is more to this than mere composition.

In real life if we were to share the concentration and intensity of the dog's head and the rabbit's eye, everything else would be out of focus. Consequently, detail on the dog's flanks would be reduced. McLean has done exactly that, reducing the detail to a superb, impressionistic rendering of muscle. Relative to the viewer's focal point the feet of both the dog and the rabbit are moving faster than the bodies themselves. McLean has, therefore, transformed their mass into patterns of colour. The outline of the dog's tail, for example, trails off into virtual transparency. Here, colour is the vehicle that is used to heighten the sense of movement. By choosing the same range of colours for both the dog and the vegetation through which he is running, he integrates all the elements into one coherent whole. The dividing line between the form and the environment fades visually into insignificance. The unaided eye again refuses to accept this lack of definition, because the brain knows there are countless fundamental differences between the dog and the dried grasses and small leaves through which he is running. If, however, a hole is cut out of a large piece of paper and placed over the tail in the painting (or print), thereby allowing a circle of colour to show through separated from its surroundings, the dividing line between the end of the tail and the rest of the background disappears. The same holds true where the back and underparts of the rabbit meet the vegetation.

But a Golden Labrador is meant to be golden, and the surroundings are not. Such expert handling of colour cannot come straight from the tube of casein. Textures have to be built up through judicious use of various shades. Too much detail would freeze the moment, and truth would be lost. As can be seen, colour in nature is frequently less important than pattern.

Many animals – but not birds – are colour-blind. McLean's *White-tailed Deer with Fawns* drives the point forcibly home. Even with our own highly developed colour perception we do not immediately pick out the fawns. The light filtering down through the canopy dapples the forest floor with

patterns that echo the spotted coats of the two young deer. It would have been more orthodox to have the fawns posed boldly against a contrasting background. Such an approach, of course, is an insult to nature. Similarly, in McLean's *Ruffed Grouse and Second Hardwood Growth*, the birds and trees are painted from the same palette.

The grouse are coloured and patterned the way they are by nature expressly so that they will not be seen. This is the gist of Abbott Thayer's theories of *Concealing Coloration in the Animal Kingdom*, which appeared under that title in book form in 1909. The sub-title was *An Exposition of the Laws of Disguise Through Color and Pattern*. Thayer considered the Ruffed Grouse the 'perfect example... the very consummation of the obliterative principle.... Nature has, as it were, used the bird's visually unsubstantialized body as a canvas on which to paint a forest vista.'

However, Thayer unreasonably insisted that the theory of concealing colouration applied to every species under every condition. His art training and his artist's eye put him, in his own opinion, above mere naturalists whom he dismissed as not qualified to understand, let alone question, his then radical theories. Thayer became obsessed with the science of colour at the expense of art, which was a shame, because his few extant watercolours show that he could have become a truly great landscape artist.

But Thayer had forced all artists to face a complex dilemma. Should birds be shown as isolated feathered maps, or would they blend and interact with the background? From an artist's point of view, Thayer's thesis had one serious limitation. If you followed it too slavishly, you would not see the bird at all. A compromise was unavoidable.

No one was plagued by this essential debate more than Thayer's great pupil, Louis Agassiz Fuertes (1874-1927). The editors of *National Geographic Magazine* and *Bird Lore* commissioned many paintings but kept on sending the work back because they felt the birds did not stand out enough from the background. 'Uncle Abbott,' as Fuertes affectionately called Thayer, constantly complained that the birds stood out far too much. To resolve the conflicting needs of publisher and artist, Fuertes evolved two styles. In his true paintings, as opposed to his illustrations, he tended to pattern himself on Uncle Abbott. At all times, however, he strove successfully to capture the personality of an individual bird, and in this he has had more influence on modern wildlife artists than any other North American since Audubon.

Most modern painters, no doubt responding to a perceived demand for accuracy as epitomized by the field guide approach so brilliantly established by Roger Tory Peterson, have opted for colour as a means of observation rather than obscurity. McLean, in his *Evening Grosbeak*, can give the colour patterns which stand out boldly from the background, but usually he adopts the views of Thayer and Fuertes rather than Peterson. He shows his *Snowy Owl* flying low against a snow covered field, not against a blue sky; he will integrate a Ring-necked Pheasant with the patterns and textures of the forest floor as seen from above, not against the sky as seen from gun sights.

Exactly what colour is a Red-winged Blackbird? To generations of art students the answer would have been found by checking in A.H. Munsell's *Atlas of the Munsell Color System* of 1913 and subsequent editions, in which the hue, value and chroma defined the three-dimensionality of colour as surely, to Munsell at least, as height, length and width defined the dimensions of a box. Most animal painters, knowingly or not, paint with Munsell's approach to colour. What they fail to appreciate is that the dimensions of a box give no hint of the material of which the box is made. Munsell assumed that colour was pigment; today, we know that it is a lot more complex than that. Depending on the material, light will react to give totally different effects. Munsell could never have reduced iridescence to fit his shorthand notation. It was not until the late 1950s that Crawford Greenewalt, working with electron microscopes, demonstrated in his epic *Hummingbirds* that the cross sections of the barbs of the feathers act as prisms which reflect and refract the sunlight to create the explosion of colour we associate with the gorgette of this species. The same phenomenon explains the rainbow hues on the neck of pigeons and the shimmering body of a grackle. The effect can only be seen within a narrowly defined triangulation in which the bird, the sun and the viewer must be lined up precisely.

The feathers of many birds not only carry pigmentation, but by their structure also act as reflectors of light. Colours are enhanced, changed or even neutralized to such a degree that only a whiteness is apparent. In McLean's marvellous painting *Red-winged Blackbird and Cattails*, the black shoulder and both the red and yellow of the epaulette reflect a white highlight. Similarly, in his extraordinary portrait of the dishevelled crow he shows how light bounces off the glossy black to obliterate the black pigment, replacing it with brilliance. Both birds are monuments to McLean's understanding of colour. Specifically, he never uses black – except in the making of another colour – nor does he use white. He understands that shadows are usually purple, snow is never white, and that there is a greenish cast to the shadowed underside of a bright red bird. That some surfaces absorb rather than reflect colour is made obvious by the textural treatment of the birds compared with that of the shaggy branch or the brown velvet of the cattails.

The role of light in creating an ambient atmosphere is frequently ignored, but it can be the dominant factor in determining the colour values on all surfaces. In McLean's early morning scene of the American elk, the upland meadow is bathed in purple, and everything within the purview of that shadow has purple overtones. This blending minimizes the significance of the animals while the strong morning rays spotlight the far peak. In such a setting, the grandeur of the mountains, and the very scale of the meadows and the sky become the main emphasis. As they are in *their* world, the Wapiti are merely co-stars. The dominant influence is the atmosphere.

Atmosphere can also mean wind direction, temperature, and moisture in the air. It can mean a spring thaw or a hard frost, and the way in which both such occurrences affect the texture of snow.

McLean paints wind. The Red-wing stretches a leg on uncooperative stalks, the wings and feathers are slightly ruffled, and the seeds escaping from the mature catkin waft away under the tug of the air. Across the field of vision, a green leaf arches in subtle response to the wind. His study of the two Red-tailed hawks carries the sense of wind even further. The bird that approaches face on is using her wings to counteract the cross wind while the male faces the air stream to reduce its influence. His centre of gravity is slightly forward of where it would be if he were at rest in still air. And, ever so artfully, McLean has painted the upward sweep of the needles of the pine top. Across the sky, clouds that have been broken up by the wind scud their way. The similarity between this painting and several created by Liljefors is absolutely uncanny.

In his *Eastern Bluebirds and Cornflowers* painting, the summer haze softens the outlines of the trees on the horizon, and adds a halo of light around the reflection off the metal roof of the barn. His Short-eared Owl ghosts in over fields where the black earth has begun to absorb sufficient warmth to speed the melting of the snow. The snow itself is soggy in anticipation of the warming days ahead. The earth would not support a footfall for the first few inches, but ice grips the foundation. The examples of atmosphere are as numerous as McLean's paintings.

We were walking, waist deep through Joe-Pye-weed and orchard grass down to the bottom land below McLean's house. Walter's Creek flowed under the rotting logs of an old bridge that once carried a road between farms that have long since reverted to nature. The early morning sun glinted off the clean water as it hurried on to Georgian Bay. The air was crisp with the fragrance of the wild mint that was bruised by our steps.

McLean stooped to examine a weathered cedar root. The patterns of the grain and the weathered textures were stored in his mental inventory. 'This is my favourite place,' he said. 'It changes every day, and I can always find new and beautiful things. Next week the dandelions will be finished and we'll get the first chicory and mullein will be in blossom. There's so much here that my biggest problem is finding enough time to use it all.' Up in the studio there had been painted studies of this land with the leaves, plants, roots and mushrooms.

Nothing in McLean's paintings is embellished. The mountains are not grander than in real life, the eagle's mien no more fierce, the trees no more towering, the colours no more vivid or the storms more threatening. He never paints more than he sees, but what he sees he understands deeply. 'You can't improve on nature!' he says. 'Either something has innate excellence or it doesn't. If it does, it's not because of anything you can add. Look at that house of ours.' The warming sun bathed the cut stones in yellow light. The classic proportions and the pitch

of the roof were right, and the builders, a century and a half ago, needed no architect or design school to pass judgment. 'The place was derelict when we bought it,' he continued, 'but it was inherently good. By rebuilding we didn't improve it; the most we could hope for was to be able to restore some of its original vigour.'

Vigour is the passion of McLean and his work. His birds and mammals, his flowers and fields, his wind and sky all sing the song of Ecclesiasticus: 'All the works of the Lord are good....' In McLean's art, the 'Dominion over...' of Genesis is overcome by the majesty of nature herself. Man is not in control. He is only left with awe.

PAINTINGS FROM THE WILD

*with notes
by George McLean*

Red-tailed Hawk Mantling

I remember painting this wintery picture right in the heart of a hot summer. I wished it was winter and that I could take a walk along one of our stone fences to see how the moss and lichen poke through the snow. Winter was far off though, so I used what reference material I could find and a large measure of memory and imagination. The patterns made by the light, rock, moss and lichen were the items I needed to orchestrate, and having done similar things before didn't make the problem any easier.

The hawk is in a 'mantling' attitude, a posture I find exciting and one that is common to many of the birds of prey. They do this after they have made a kill, spreading their wings to cover and protect their victim. I haven't shown what it is the hawk has killed, leaving that part to the imagination of the viewer. Anyone who is familiar with these birds will know what my hawk is doing even though no element of the actual prey is visible.

BALD EAGLE

The Bald Eagle is the only eagle confined to America, one good reason for its rank as national bird of the U.S.A. Once widely established, the Bald Eagle has been severely restricted over most of its former range by pesticide poisoning and is abundant only on the Pacific coast of B.C. and Alaska. Bald Eagles are a form of sea eagle, preferring to scavenge the shores of the ocean, lakes and rivers for dead fish. Where carrion fish are unavailable, the eagles prey on ducks, shore birds and small mammals. Occasionally, they catch live fish for themselves but will seize any opportunity to steal them from Osprey hawks, who are better fishers.

The nest, or 'aerie,' is located high in a large tree or on an inaccessible cliff face. A variety of heavy sticks, twigs, turf, seaweed, etcetera, make up the nest, which is lined with grass. The aeries are used years on end. Each year, new material is added until the nest assumes huge proportions, sometimes measuring more than ten feet deep.

Bald eagles mate for life, both sexes taking part in the nest building and care of their young. There are normally two eaglets hatched, but they compete for food and the larger of the two will sometimes bully and starve the other to death. A curious phenomenon occurs in that the young are noticeably larger than their parents for the first year after leaving the aerie, their wing span exceeding that of the adults, sometimes by a foot or more.

Eagles are splendid birds – wondrous in flight, powerfully built and fierce of countenance, they make attractive models. But, subjects with such electric personalities must be portrayed with restraint – all that is sentimental must be omitted, leaving only the raw, poetic beauty that is naturally an eagle's. If my Bald Eagle portrait is a success, it is because I held these thoughts in mind when I painted it.

Bald Eagle

McLean – 2/76

CANADA GEESE AND GOSLINGS

Paintings of animals with their young often tend to be sentimental or romantic, and I try to avoid this problem when preparing my preliminary studies for such a picture. The behaviour of the adult birds as compared to the young is important in this picture. The mature geese are alert and watchful as their pretty young ones trail along behind, apparently oblivious to the dangers that threaten, yet staying close to the parent birds.

This painting was done for some friends who own a superb small lake nearby my home. My friends raised some Canada geese there a few years ago, but when fall came, some of them flew off and went south, only to return the next spring to raise their own families. The flock has grown yearly so that there are always several families living there each summer. They can often be seen on the lake or grazing on the lawn near the water, but always retreat to the lake if one tries to approach them.

The painting hangs on a wall near a large window which overlooks the lake below. In the winter, when the lake is frozen and lifeless, the painting is a friendly reminder that summer isn't all that far off.

Canada Geese and Goslings

CROW ON BEECH LIMB

In spite of his wicked reputation, I like and admire the Crow. Crows have a pervasive, mysterious aura that seems to heighten their intelligent character. Totally black from beak to foot and elegantly proportioned, the Crow is a dignified looking bird. He is omnivorous, his daily fare consisting of insects, mice, other small mammals and young birds. Nor is he adverse to scavenging. He has been accused of enjoying eggs – but who doesn't? Most of his diet, however, is vegetarian, corn being a special favourite. Farmers concoct a bizarre collection of 'scarecrows' to fend him off, but still he persists.

Because of his excesses, the Crow has been persecuted. Only his native intelligence and wary disposition saves him from annihilation. He has been lured by hunters with imitation crow-calls and owl decoys, to be shot at, poisoned and even dynamited on his roost when all else fails. For sheer excess, the Crow could take lessons from his human tormentors.

Gregarious birds except at nesting time, crows gather in flocks to migrate, sometimes thousands strong. Noisy birds most of the time, they often collect to shout at and annoy their enemies, hawks and owls. While they raise their young, however, they live silent, secluded lives, building a sturdy nest of sticks lined with strips of bark, in a high tree. There are four to seven eggs, pale green or blue and spotted brown. The young have ravenous appetites, consuming over half their weight daily. Easily tamed, they make good pets and can be taught to talk. But they are extremely curious and have an impudent way of stealing anything they can lift. My painting shows one in an attitude that, to me, exemplifies his curious, alert, somewhat mysterious nature.

Crow on Beech Limb

McLeon - 6/71

EASTERN BLUEBIRDS

SKETCH OF EASTERN BLUEBIRDS IN FOG   EASTERN BLUEBIRDS AND CORNFLOWERS

Several years ago, I was commissioned to paint a picture for the Canadian Arthritis Society using their emblem, the bluebird, as a subject. I hadn't painted many songbirds and was remarkably uninterested in the project. However, I decided to give it a try. I borrowed a pair of study skins from the Royal Ontario Museum and set out to find some appropriate background to place the birds in.

I made two coloured sketches, each quite different from the other. Often, when I give a client two sketches to choose from, he picks the one I would least like to paint. In this instance I didn't mind which one they chose and as it turned out they decided on *Eastern Bluebirds and Cornflowers*. I intend to make a finished picture of this remaining sketch some day soon, because, having done the first painting, I have found a way of portraying small birds that intrigues me. It pays sometimes to extend oneself and to explore new areas even though they may be of little interest at the outset.

Bluebirds were, at one time, a much more common sight than they are today. The introduction of aggressive species, such as House Sparrows and Starlings, who prefer similiar nesting sites, contributed to their decline. Still, I sometimes see them sitting on a fence or overhead powerline and am always delighted by their cheery appearance. In an effort to encourage them to nest nearby, I have set out birdhouses with entrances large enough for bluebirds but too small for their competitors – however, to date, only some affable swallows have used them.

The moody, monochromatic softness of a late summer day provided a complimentary setting for the bluebirds. The wild asters and chicory, interspersed with goldenrod, add colour to an otherwise grey setting; the birds and cornflowers combine to support the overall blue theme of this painting.

Months before starting this picture, I did the background studies, not knowing then how I would use them but eventually the birds were added to my preliminary sketch. Winter had set in with a vengeance before I got around to the finished work. At one point, I was snowbound for 10 days as my

picture developed. The painting provided a gentle reminder that winter's storms would end; the birds and flowers would come again.

The bluebirds were treated as part of the scenery, embroidered, as it were, into their environment. They are of central interest but the detail in the feathers is more an impression of feathers than a tightly controlled rendering. The same is true of the weeds in the foreground. Each species, though readily identifiable, is handled as part of the whole.

Sketch of
Eastern Bluebirds
in Fog

Eastern Bluebirds and Cornflowers

EVENING GROSBEAK

I have commented often that gesture is of supreme importance to me in an animal picture. By this I mean that particular aspect of a pose that gives the animal life and character. The pose may represent intense action or some subtle nuance of motion that readily identifies the species yet adds some freshness to an otherwise ordinary stance. My Grosbeak falls into the second category and I chose the bird's attitude with care.

The background was also carefully considered as to design and placement of the apples, among other things. The branch and apples came from my friend and neighbour's apple orchard. The grosbeaks seem not to eat the fruit, just the seeds and I think I know why. When I brought the apples into the studio they thawed out and filled the house with an aroma akin to that of the locker room at the gymnasium (or cider vinegar!).

Every winter, several species of birds come to the feeders outside my studio window. I enjoy them all but especially the brightly coloured grosbeaks. No matter how violent the weather, they come and provide a bright spot of colour to help drive away my winter feeling of isolation. Last winter I fed them 550 lbs of sunflower seeds in exchange for the pleasure of their company.

Evening Grosbeak

McLean - 4/73

GOLDEN EAGLE AND PREY

My first intention here was to make a simple portrait of this rather belligerent looking eagle with only the beech limb for a background. In fact, that is precisely what my sketch shows. However, the more I developed the finished eagle, the more certain I became that the painting needed some other element to explain its aggressive expression. The strength of most design is simplicity but especially in a vignette. So it was with reluctance that I added the dead pheasant.

One other consideration in adding the pheasant was the knowledge that some people have a curious, somewhat amusing dislike of portraits of dead things. What I find amusing is that no one would be offended by a Norman Rockwell illustration depicting a New England family gathered together for their traditional Thanksgiving turkey dinner!

The pheasant was provided for me by a friend nearby who raises pheasants for the poultry market. However, most of my dead models are fresh animals killed either on the road or through some other accident. I keep the specimens frozen in plastic bags, sometimes for years. When I need to refer to one, I simply thaw it out until I am finished with it, then refreeze it for future use. I find dead specimens far superior to the stiff, dry museum skins that bear little resemblance to a live animal.

Golden Eagle and Prey

McLean

GREAT HORNED OWL

SKETCH OF OWL AND
EASTERN GREY SQUIRREL

GREAT HORNED OWL AND JACKRABBIT

Action pictures of this nature are demanding, the ones I have the most difficulty with, and also the ones I find most satisfying if they succeed. The squirrel has barely escaped his attacker, a Great Horned Owl, and will soon vanish into the safety of the pine woods. Cropping the owl's wings was a decision I arrived at to give the feeling of crowding, the sensation the squirrel must feel as he desperately plunges into space. Also, I tried to place the animals in attitudes that are striking, yet believable, conveying the urgency of the moment.

At the time of this writing, I am working on the finished painting of this sketch. I have both a dead owl and a dead squirrel to act as models. The owl was caught in a pole trap by a neighbour whose poultry he had been killing, and the squirrel is one I found dead on the road. Also, I have some sketches of a dead squirrel that I made at about the age of 15. Although the paper is tattered and smudged, the drawings are good enough for reference. There is no substitute for a good field sketch.

Sundown beckons; the Great Horned Owl drops from his hidden roost high in a hemlock to drift silently into the night, seeking out his quarry. His keen eyesight records tenuous stirrings amid the ground cover; he attacks quickly and surely, his approach muffled by dense, fluffy feathers. The kill is made with dispatch. Birds or small mammals, even skunks, may fall victim to the owl, but true to his race, he is a fearsome hunter who does what owls must to survive. That is nature's way.

Handsome birds, bristling with character, horned owls excite and intrigue me every time I see one sitting etched against the evening sky, or hear one hooting at night in the river valley below my house. Their presence often goes unnoticed, although they are fairly common and may be found inhabiting wooded ravines or parks within city limits. Though normally nocturnal and secretive, I see one now and then being harassed by songbirds or crows who set up a loud din to announce the owl's hiding place. The more agile birds will dart in to pick at and pluck out a feather or two. After dark, however, the roles are reversed; the owl, having superior eyesight, catches his prey unawares, thus earning the fear and loathing of the other birds who in the daylight are far too fast for him.

I've expediently elected to paint my Great Horned Owl in daylight. On occasion, horned owls can and do hunt very well during the day, especially while rearing their young. Contrary to common belief, their eyesight, rather than being impaired by light, is very efficient before dark.

The decision to vignette the background in this painting stems from my observation that certain animal forms are strong enough to stand by themselves, rendering a complete background superfluous. The spartan surroundings here emphasize the defiance of the owl victoriously perched on his kill – a jackrabbit.

Sketch of Owl and
Eastern Grey Squirrel

Great Horned Owl and Jackrabbit

PEREGRINE FALCON AND MEADOWLARK

The Peregrine Falcon or Duckhawk is one of the fastest birds in the sky, diving or stooping at speeds of up to 170 miles per hour. It is the only falcon with worldwide distribution and was formerly used by nobility to hunt game birds. Peregrines, though intrepid hunters, are gentle, easily taught birds, much cherished by falconers.

Before the advent of guns, falcons were used in their place. No one knows how old falconry is, but it was practised by the ancient Persians and Egyptians. The sport of falconry is carried on today, but on a much reduced scale, due in part to the drop in the falcon population. Pesticide poisoning is largely responsible for the rapid decline of many predatory bird species, the Peregrine being a good example. Never common birds, the Peregrine has been eliminated as a breeding species in much of its former range.

Peregrines habitually prey on such birds as ducks, shore birds, pigeons, grouse and larger songbirds. When hunting, the falcon selects his intended victim, circles from above until sure of his target. Then, he stoops, attacking at great speed, delivering his quarry a killing blow. Peregrines usually kill birds in mid flight, but have been known to mistakenly strike a wooden decoy of a duck with such force as to knock the decoy's head off.

Several years ago, I watched a trained Peregrine in action in western Canada – an experience that left me dumbfounded and one I will never forget. For sheer speed, aggression and agility, the Peregrine has few peers. Having watched him perform, I made this painting. My only regret is that I didn't make the painting life-size to better stress the impact of this magnificent creature on me.

Peregrine Falcon and Meadowlark

McLean – 7/70

RED-TAILED HAWK

SKETCH OF TWO RED-TAILS

SKETCH OF TWO RED-TAILS

Variations of weather and light effects contribute to the special mood of a painting. In this picture, I kept the background simple. The day is bright, the clouds torn and driven by a stiff wind. The hawk in the foreground is blown and dishevelled, clinging to its perch in the wind, watching its mate struggle through the gale.

I have used several devices to suggest wind in this painting: the sprig of pine bending, the birds' feathers in disarray, and the tattered clouds, suggesting motion. The element of wind is intended to dramatize this scene and the arrangement of the composition designed to create a feeling of stress.

In each picture I try to inject a mood or feeling that brings a uniqueness to it. Sometimes it may be a feeling of surprise or perhaps that feeling of awe that comes when seeing something clearly that could normally only be glimpsed.

RED-TAILED HAWK AND STARLINGS

Much constraint must be exercised by an artist in portraying animals in action. The animals need to be understood, both physically and psychologically. An element of action can add excitement to a painting or become a tacky device. The success of a picture hinges on a good idea plus technical excellence, no matter what the attitude of the animal.

I began this painting as a portrait of a huge white pine. The tree established a dominant shape to which, with some editing, I added the hawk and starlings. I used the birds to create an illusion of chaotic motion that would be gone in a flash, leaving only the landscape, empty once more. Also, the paint was applied somewhat impressionistically, to further aid the illusion of speed.

This species of hawk does not usually hunt small birds because they are too quick to catch. The Red-tails' prey is predominantly rodents; mice, squirrels and ground squirrels, but when opportunity permits, birds.

According to scientific classification, Red-tails are *buteo* or broad-winged hawks who ride the winds, watching with telescopic vision, for any likely trophy. Another hunting technique employed by these hawks is to fly low over a field of long grass, striking animals caught off guard. Out of my studio window, I have seen one sit on a dead snag, waiting for a vole and then, suddenly, stoop, catch his victim and return to his perch to eat. I find the interrelationship of animals irresistibly attractive, particularly that relationship between a hunter and hunted. I never tire of painting them.

Red-tailed Hawk

Sketch of Two Red-tailed Hawks

Red-tailed Hawk and Starlings

Red-tailed Hawk on Maple Limb

Red-tailed hawks may be seen any day of the year where I live. No matter, they are always to be admired and appreciated. Sitting hunched against a winter gale or floating listless on a summer sky, they lend a character that is almost spiritual, a part of the countryside.

My vignette is designed to impart this vitality through the careful use of large shapes. That which is left out of a good picture is as significant as that which has been put in. Howard Pyle, the American illustrator and teacher, suggested that a picture, well designed, should draw attention even when the viewer is too far away to make sense of the drawing or subject. The attitude of my hawk is one I've never seen used before and one that I hope corresponds to Pyle's remark.

My use of shape is guided as much by what looks right as by what is correct. One general criticism I have of many animal paintings is the lack of imagination used in selecting expressive poses. Photography, while not the complete answer, offers endless opportunities for shapes not worn out through overuse.

Red-tails lead flamboyant lives that provide many possibilities for pictures. What fostered my idea for this picture was an experience I had one winter day as I walked out for the mail. My lane is long, bordered by maple trees. There was a bitter breeze that made a rustling in the leaves still clinging to some of the branches, but not much other sound. Then, surprisingly, a hawk I hadn't noticed spread his wings and coasted out across the field. I wished he had stayed longer, so that I could get a better look at him – but he was gone. However, I remembered and brought him back in my picture.

RED-WINGED BLACKBIRD AND CATTAILS

Wind, water, cattails; a Red-wing stretching in the morning sun; the fragrance of poplar trees; timeless symbols of spring and the marsh. Just before winter releases its icy grip, the Red-wings return, their welcome cheery song of *o-ka-lee!* can be heard, proclaiming their arrival and summoning warmer weather.

Red-winged blackbirds, in days past, restricted themselves to wetlands, riversides and the like, but have extended their range, and now they are seen anywhere they can nest and find enough to eat. Hardy, prolific birds, as are most species of blackbirds, they are deemed a nuisance in parts of the west where huge flocks sometimes gather to descend on grain fields. However, almost all of their food is made up of weed seeds or insects harmful to agriculture. It might be truthfully said that Red-wings are beneficial to man except when overabundant. Of course, one could also say that of man himself.

The Red-wing builds a nest suspended two or three feet from the ground in reeds, sedge or low bushes. Three to six pale green or blue eggs, each finely spotted dark brown, except for a heavier band of spots at the large extremity, are laid in a nest of woven grass.

I recall making a preliminary sketch of this painting which didn't quite suit me. However, I went ahead with the finished work, painting in the bird, the reeds and cattails, but the same nagging doubts prevailed. I had the cattails in my studio and portrayed them just as they were when I cut them, tiny spider-web included, but the picture remained incomplete. Exasperated, after weeks of work and thought, I took a short hike one afternoon. I soon discovered some bulrushes and knew they were the perfect addition to my nearly completed work. I painted one seedy spike of that plant, without which the picture was a nonentity.

Red-winged Blackbird and Cattails

McLean-10/72

RING-NECKED PHEASANT

A cock pheasant, luminous in the sunlight, struts warily through the undercover. The fallen leaves cushion his step, ferns and shaggy-mane mushrooms line his way. A perfect gem, resplendent in a fairyland collage of colour.

The Ring-neck would sooner walk or run than fly and though he is gloriously decorated, he can dissolve into his habitat like magic. But, his boisterous cackle gives him away as he proclaims his territory and issues a challenge to other males of his stock. Huntsmen also hear the challenge and each year an army of them stalk the fields and hedgerows with their trained dogs to bag a brace or two of wild pheasants for their tables.

Introduced to North America from China in the early 1880s, pheasants have become so well established that millions of them are killed annually by hunters in Canada and the United States. Pheasant hatcheries help to maintain the pheasant population by restocking. Deep snow in the area where I live won't allow pheasants to scratch for food as they must. In these circumstances, restocking each year is the only way to provide enough birds for hunting.

The henbird, unlike her mate, is modestly coloured a mottled brown. She makes her nest often in open fields, but sometimes in brush where she hides nearly invisible as she incubates her clutch of ten or twelve greenish-brown eggs. As they hatch, the newborn downy young can follow the hen, feeding themselves on seeds and insects. The parent bird defends them from predators as best she can and shelters them from the cold. The young birds remain with the hen until full grown.

Ring-necked Pheasant

RUFFED GROUSE

SKETCH OF GROUSE EGGS

The forest floor, laden with a host of riches, is trampled but rarely noticed by those who travel its paths. Every moss-covered root or decaying stump has a character all its own, and will harbour an array of live things, small but beautiful. A careful examination of the woodland flora reveals a world at once familiar, yet ultimately foreign, dazzling in all its colour and texture. There are times when I would rather paint a square yard of the earth's surface than the grandest mountain range.

That may explain my enthusiasm for painting the grouse nest and eggs. Just a hollow spot at the base of a tree is all the hen needs for her large clutch of eggs. A few select leaves and feathers for lining compose the unpretentious structure. A fragile jewel settled in an austere world.

One day, a covey of baby grouse will emerge from these eggs. Within a week they will be able to fly enough to reach the safety of a low tree branch. At least some of them will be taken by predators; a fox or owl, perhaps a weasel. But life and death are synonymous with nature – enough will survive to perpetuate their kind.

Nests fascinate me. I have painted several of them and don't think I'm being repetitious. Every one is a work of art on its own, always with its innate charm and lovely design. My real interest is in capturing that which is temporary and preserving it, faithfully, as it was when I saw it.

STUDY OF FOREST FLOOR

For an artist, no photograph, however good, can supply the intimate understanding of an object that a drawing from life can. That even applies to field sketches that are unsuccessful, because the level of observation for any sketch is many times greater than for that of a photo. Photographs are useful references but without proper field experience, the artist who uses photographs exclusively will only reproduce his reference material, never making his own unique statement.

This sketch of the woodland floor is typical of the sketches I make outdoors. I usually record the details rather than the wide panoramic view. Often I photograph the spot I painted to later compare the accuracy of my observations. Although the photos sometimes reveal errors in drawing, the exercise of

Sketch of Grouse Eggs

Study of Forest Floor

Ruffed Grouse and Jack-in-the-Pulpit

RUFFED GROUSE
AND JACK-IN-THE-PULPIT

working from life allows me to work without photographs when they are unavailable.

Working outdoors, for me, has a wonderful therapeutic effect. As I sit working quietly, I often see wild creatures before they have seen me. Also, the experience of weather and the seasons is felt profoundly, both physically and visually, while working in the field. The scent of mouldy leaves, the feel of a chill autumn day, or the sounds of birds chattering and singing are all a bonus to the artist who disciplines himself to work from life outdoors.

The Ruffed Grouse is so called because of the dark, iridescent ruff of feathers around its neck. Both sexes exhibit the ruff but the male, in its courtship display, spreads his ruff and tail while drooping his wings, bowing and strutting, before his intended mate. The display postures are exquisite and occur throughout the late winter and early spring. My painting shows a displaying grouse, surrounded by plant life indigenous to his northeastern range, including a Jack-in-the-Pulpit.

Ruffed Grouse are favoured upland game birds, widely distributed in the northern hemisphere. The curious 'drumming' habit of the cockbirds, particularly in the spring, sets them apart from other grouse species. The male selects a log or other elevation, sits back on his fanned tail and begins, slowly at first, then picking up speed, beating the air with his wings to produce a drumming sound. This is thought to be a challenge and warning to other cocks to keep off his territory.

A characteristic introduction to the grouse may happen on a casual walk through the woods where they live. Rendered quite invisible by his protective colouration, the grouse lies motionless until almost stepped upon. His startling, explosive flight at the last moment is unnerving – his retreat to safety swift. This elusive behaviour makes the Ruffed Grouse much sought after by sportsmen, and taxes every man's skill as a marksman.

Grouse live in hilly, wooded country broken by open fields or swampy woodlands. The bulk of their food is vegetable but they eat insects as well. In winter they live primarily on buds, certain of which (i.e. white cedar) render their flesh unpalatable. Also, in winter Ruffed Grouse develop stubby, hair-like projections around their toes to help support themselves on the snow.

RUFFED GROUSE AND SECOND HARDWOOD GROWTH

Camouflage is one of the elements of animal painting that interests me most. No bird blends into its surroundings better than the Ruffed Grouse and that is the object of this painting. Even though the grouse are in the foreground, they are not easy to see.

I remember finding a grouse nest at the base of a tree a couple of years ago. I decided to make a picture of it so I gathered up my equipment and wandered over to the spot where the nest was located. I walked to within a few feet of it but all I could see were the dried leaves around the tree roots. I could hardly believe my eyes so I took another step forward. Suddenly, there was a terrific explosion as the 'invisible' hen flew up and sped off into the surrounding cover of woods. Without the marvellous camouflage of the mother bird, the eggs were obvious and vulnerable, so I did my work and retreated with haste.

The background for my painting of the grouse was done near Elmvale, Ontario, where I once lived. The pine tree was growing alongside the highway, amid a young forest of second growth hardwood. I suppose the pine had been spared the ax because the log was too short, but it made a good model, massive in contrast to all those slender maples. The tree remains, although the road has since been raised and one can barely see it now.

RUFFED GROUSE DISPLAYING

Some birds lend themselves to picture-making more than others. Sometimes the bird's traditional relationship to man makes it interesting. Perhaps its behaviour and form distinguish it or maybe it's just a very beautiful creature that ought to be painted for no other reason than that. I admire the Grouse for all these characteristics.

The idea for this picture was conceived late last winter on a walk through the woods. Spring's leisurely approach was melting the snow. Grouse tracks were etched into the crystalline snow, which still lay deep wherever it was shaded by the trees. Where the snow had withdrawn, the forest floor was sodden, the vegetation dark and baroque in all its sombre detail.

First I made a detailed pencil sketch of the Grouse, next a rough charcoal drawing integrating bird and landscape. Then I went to work on the finished painting. The final work took several weeks, and occasionally, I'd walk into the valley to check some important detail or other. By the time my painting was complete, all the leaves had come on the trees. Summer had arrived.

I've treated this painting as a vignette, using the white of the panel as the snow. In doing this it was necessary to keep the light flat because any suggestion of strong light would have coloured the snow, thus losing the vignette effect.

Ruffed Grouse and Second Hardwood Growth

Ruffed Grouse Displaying

McLean

SHORT-EARED OWL LANDING

One needn't attend an avant-garde art museum to find and enjoy exciting abstract shapes and patterns; they are everywhere abundant in nature. My attention to this picture was first aroused at the textured patterns made in the snow by the bared plough furrows. The contrast between dark earth and the comparatively bright snow creates a simple, somewhat abstract landscape. The contorted form of the owl augments the severe surroundings, yet offers a focal point.

The great abstractionist painters ignore draughtsmanship to better concentrate on non-objective form. Their inventive use of texture, pattern and design are inspiring to anyone concerned with picture-making. Whether the format be non-objective or realistic, the basic precepts of picture construction are the same. Those of us who like to draw simply add one more dimension.

The thrill of seeing any wild animal undisturbed at its daily task is something that I love to share through my pictures. Even though mood and feelings are abstract entities, difficult to define, I attempt to do this when I paint, something I'm sure I share with all true artists, no matter what their personal means of self-expression.

On the ground, the Short-eared Owl is practically invisible. I have been pleasantly surprised several times when a Short-ear suddenly and noiselessly fluttered up from the grass nearby to drift off across the open fields. Because they live in open country and regularly hunt in daylight, these are the owls most commonly seen skimming the grass, watching and listening for mice and other small animals.

Short-eared Owl Landing

CHARLES

CHARLES IN THE GRASS

In springs past, when most of the snow was gone, and the dead grass lay flattened by winter's onslaught, Charlie, our house-cat, would roam the fields, catching mice. This was a wonderful time of year for Charles. She loathed the cold weather and heavy snow but once the run-off came, many of the rodents would be flooded out of their burrows and Charlie would go hunting. Sometimes she would catch so many mice, she couldn't eat them all. So she'd bring them home and leave them on the verandah for a later snack.

In this study, I've shown the cat watching, attentively poised to spring at just the right moment. Charlie was beautifully marked in a tortoise-shell pattern and she made a fine model. The colour of her white and grey coat, contrasted against the sombre grass, always appealed to me.

Now that Charlie is gone, spring isn't quite the same. Even now, I find myself taking a second look at a distant patch of snow and wondering absent-mindedly, if it's the cat.

CHARLES ON THE WOODPILE

Charlie came to stay with us when she was only a few weeks old. Turned out that Charles was a female and she didn't take long to let us know it. She raised a litter of four kittens before she was a year old. She was extraordinary in many ways. Handsome, gentle and intelligent, she often accompanied me on hikes when I'd go out to paint. That is how I came to make this, the first painting I ever made of her.

Of all the drawings and paintings I did using Charlie as a model, this is my favourite. She was infinitely curious – first looking into this rockpile or that clump of weeds, next climbing the fence for a better overall view, always testing the wind for smells known only to herself. I tried to capture some of that character and curiosity in Charlie's inquisitive pose.

This painting was quite a diversion for me back in 1969. Really, I did it just as an exercise and didn't attach much importance to it. In fact, neither did my dealer in those days, Budd Feheley. He asked me why the hell I was wasting my time doing pictures of no interest to anyone but me. And yet, after both Budd and I took a closer look and had a chance to digest it, we agreed it was an interesting avenue to try.

Charlie lived almost 14 years. She was an outstanding character and although I miss her, I'm glad to have known her.

Charles in the Grass

Charles on the Woodpile

COUGAR RECLINING IN TREE

All cats fascinate me but none more than the cougar. I've dealt with this exquisite subject in several earlier works, always trying to emphasize the supple, yet powerful form. My approach to picture-making has developed into a philosophy of understatement, frequently leaving something unsaid. In this painting I wanted to convey a subtle self-confidence accompanying the lazy posture of the big cat, never betraying his hidden potential for violence.

What prompted this picture was a small landscape I painted on a trip made years ago through the Rockies. A forest fire was smouldering somewhere in the valley, emitting a stench and smoke screen that could be seen and smelled for miles. The trees, silhouetted against the foggy (smoky) background reminded me of a Japanese woodcut. At first, I was tempted to show a group of small birds being pursued by a hawk; then came a better, fresher thought – the cougar.

The use of landscape material is of paramount importance to the success of any animal painting. No matter how convincingly the animal is drawn, a poor background will render it unbelievable. That is why I chose this setting for the mountain lion – he belongs there.

Cats of all species make good models but the cougar is a favourite of mine. The relatively small head, mounted on a great, muscular body, lends a classical presence, always a pleasure to paint. Most cats like a high perch where they are safe and can see what goes on around them, sometimes dozing in the sun. Such is the case in this picture.

Study of Trees

Sketch of Cougar

Cougar

Cougar Reclining in Tree

GOLDEN LAB RETRIEVER

Generally, I tend to reject commissions involving pet portraits, but this was an exception. I agreed to paint this picture because I admired the dog and enjoyed his friendly disposition. Also, my client gave me free rein to paint the picture in any way I chose.

Labs were originally bred to retrieve waterfowl. This particular dog is not trained to hunt, but will, like most healthy dogs, chase rabbits, so that is the way I portrayed him. The setting is similar to that where the dog lives, although I designed it myself, rather than painting it from a specific location. The arrangement of light and undergrowth was designed to give an illusion of motion and camouflage.

This is not really a life-and-death struggle between dog and rabbit. The rabbit will outrun his pursuer with ease and the dog knows it from experience. My point here was to demonstrate the dog's good nature, typical of his race, and his vigorous means of showing it.

101

Golden Lab Retriever

LIONESS

As a lad I used to dream of going to Africa to
see the wildlife there. I read stories about
that continent and envied the men who saw
it as it was in the past – teeming with game
and full of adventure. I may go to Africa some
day but I know it won't be as thrilling as I
once envisioned. The land has changed and
many of the animals, once so abundant,
are almost totally gone. Maybe that is why I
don't paint many African subjects though
I do enjoy painting the big, exotic cats now
and again.

This picture was based on a photograph
that my artist friend, Bob Bateman, gave me.
I have shown considerably more of the lion
than was in the photo, but the photo is what
sparked the idea. The bright African sun
warming the lioness and the clear blue sky
were what gave me my first incentive. I
added the vultures later, suggesting, perhaps,
that she is resting after a hearty meal, otherwise unseen in the picture.

YOUNG LIONESS

The facial expressions of lions and the
resulting personality they communicate vary
as much as do those of humans. Head proportions make some lions handsome, others
less attractive models. Some artists tend to
paint certain types of lion almost without
exception. Wilhelm Kuhnert, the famous
German painter of African animals, chose to
paint long-nosed lions with relatively
small chins. Of course, there are variations in
all the mammal species and it is possible
to select the best looking from the rest in each
case. My personal concern is more oriented
towards individuals than general types,
although one tends to choose specimens that
look normal and healthy.

My lion portrait shows a young, robust
lioness whose attention is directed at some
distant object. The lines of her face are still
soft, her eyes large in proportion to the
rest of her head. Also, her head is large in
relation to her body as are her feet – all signs
of her immaturity. But she has already
outgrown many of her clumsy, kittenish
features and will soon emerge a sleek, powerful animal well able to support herself.

Lioness and Vultures

Young Lioness

MOUNTAIN GOATS

I always feel mildly intimidated when confronted with the prospect of painting animals in a mountain setting – especially one with a panoramic view. Mountains are such imposing structures, I find it difficult not to say more about them in a picture than I mean to. Carl Rungius, the dean of North American big-game painters, produced hundreds of mountain pictures, and if there is a way of doing it that is better or different, I have yet to find it. So, it was with some trepidation that I decided to paint this picture of the goats.

The material for their setting was collected several years ago on a field trip to the Rocky Mountains of western Canada. The mountain range is appropriately named Sawback and is located deep in the wild interior of Alberta's Banff National Park. A friend and I drove in on a trail that was rough and periodically obscure in his worn all-terrain vehicle which, only reluctantly, responded to its mission. It displayed a feisty streak that threatened at times to roll us over and send us careening into oblivion. But, we got there and back, and in the doing had some adventure in a countryside too spectacular to describe – except in a painting.

We climbed the mountain one cold morning before the sun could rise high enough to warm the valley and melt the thick hoarfrost that coated it. An elk had been bugling from high up the slope through the night, so we set out to try and get a look at him. The walk was steep and we had removed our jackets by the time we reached the sunlight. On the way, we saw several remarkably tame ptarmigan, a form of mountain grouse, and heard their hoarse call. We also spooked elk two or three times, but never got very close to them.

However, the trek was well worth the energy spent just to look down at the great valley spread below, embossed by the silver threads that the river made as it fanned out and wove its way from the lake and glacier where it was born. Although it took years, my goat picture evolved from this experience. The painting always reminds me of the trip, the crisp mountain air and the fine companionship.

Mountain Goats

OTTER
WITH POND
LILIES

The location for this landscape is near
Algonquin Park, Ontario, where I used to do
some canoeing. Travelling by canoe took
me to beautiful places, many of them quite
wild and undamaged by civilization. Some of
the trips were more of an endurance test
than fun, but there was always the reward of
having been somewhere and having seen
things that few others had shared.

Most people enjoy water lilies and I am no
exception. The lilies floating on the crystal
water and the mossy log were what inspired
this painting. The otter came later. Of course,
in my view, no painting of mine is complete
without an animal in it and the otter seemed
like a good choice.

The otter is one of my favourite animals
and I've made other pictures of them. They
are such good-looking, active fellows, one
hardly knows how to select one pose from
another. I've shown this one typically alert
and partially in the water, where he is
perfectly at home.

Otter with Pond Lilies

PRONGHORN ANTELOPE

In historical times the antelope herds shared their territory on the prairies with the North American bison, and like the bison, their numbers were vastly reduced by the onslaught of white settlement. One of the fastest runners on earth, the Pronghorn can maintain speeds of 40 or 50 miles an hour for extended periods, sometimes sprinting up to 65 or 70 miles an hour. Fences pose a problem for the herds because they aren't high jumpers but they know their terrain – and will go through or under fences when necessary. Pronghorns run with their mouths wide open and their tongues hanging out to better facilitate their heavy breathing.

They have incredibly keen vision and sense of smell coupled with a nervous disposition. A large white patch of long hair, located on the rump, can be erected when alarmed to warn the other members of the herd who will stampede at the slightest provocation.

Pronghorn antelope aren't really antelope at all but lone members of a family that is exclusively North American. The Pronghorn's dense coat consists of rigid hairs, each of which is hollow and offers good insulation from the cold. They are missing the dew claws that accompany most hoofed animals and unlike any other horned mammal, they annually shed the outer sheath of their horns.

I've seen wild Pronghorns in the West and was surprised at how perfectly they blend into their surroundings. They are animals of the open plains that I enjoy but have not painted often. Antelope fall into the category of 'big game animals' and I am not specifically a big game painter. The customers who buy that type of picture usually want a trophy animal to adorn their walls. My concern is more with the individual animal than with the species as a whole, so I'm not adverse to painting a small imperfect set of horns, as I did in this case. I realize that there is a large audience for pictures of big game, but that has all been well done before. I'd like to make my own contribution in my personal way.

Pronghorn Antelope

RED FOXES

RED FOXES AND BEECH TREE

The locale for this picture is on the Niagara escarpment in Ontario, a wild, rugged stretch of land, over 200 miles long, which skirts the property I live on. The escarpment has a character all its own, providing an endless variety of settings such as the one I've chosen to paint. I love the gnarled, mossy root systems that beech trees often send out, but what really inspired this picture was the contrast between the massive tree and the delicate trillium blossom. In this instance, the landscape was what first excited me – the foxes followed and were an appropriate addition.

Each picture poses its own particular problems and although I've fought through similar situations many times, I have yet to find a formula that resolves any problem consistently. This picture took several weeks to paint and was fraught with difficulties concerning texture and pattern. Sometimes pictures suffer from a wealth of detail and clutter. However, I felt that this idea had value and the potential difficulties were a challenge. The key to the problem was keeping the edges soft, playing up important areas, i.e. the standing fox, while allowing the less significant areas to recede into the background.

Foxes are shy, stealthy animals, often present though seldom seen. They usually travel alone except in the spring when they mate, and both parents raise their young. I wanted to convey the typically sharp, alert personality of foxes in a lush setting – somewhat like a tapestry. Occasionally, I do a painting that I would like to keep – although I never do. This is one of them.

Red Foxes and Beech Tree

Although this sketch is seemingly a violent picture, not a pretty one, I expect to make a finished work of it some day. The reason it interests me is that it is a legitimate, unemotional portrait of a fox doing what nature prepared him for. Also, the design elements of the picture come together to produce the mood I wanted to achieve. The time of year is spring.

In this season, the snow can be seen retreating from the bases of the small poplar trees in the background. The temperature is mild, but the light is flat and cold. There has been a short chase and the predator has caught his prey. The fox isn't much larger than the jackrabbit he is killing, a fact that will come as a surprise to those who think of foxes as large animals. The struggle will be short but because of the snow, the fox is floundering and awkward.

My interest in the animals I choose to paint is total. As long as the animals are doing things that come naturally to them in their proper surroundings, chances are I'll find them interesting to paint – in action or not. I find myself painting more pictures that are difficult or impossible to photograph. I would say this is one of those.

Red Fox Running

A teacher once told me that if I could paint nothing and do it well, I would be an artist. At the time, I took issue with his comment, it seemed glib, designed to annoy as well as frustrate. However, as the years roll on, I spend most of my days pursuing that very elusive philosophy, honing my pictures to the bone.

This picture is carefully edited. The fox takes up very little space, and yet if he suddenly came to life and galloped off the panel, he would run away, taking most of my enthusiasm with him. But, it wasn't the fox I wanted to portray; rather the mood of the day and season. The fleeing fox is, perhaps, symbolic of the strange sadness I feel watching the winter retreat, even though I dread the months of isolation it imposes on me. The changing season is a marker of time, a framework for days gone and the joy or pain that gave them meaning. Though rigorous and lonely, winter has a vitality that evokes from me more of a certain energy than does any other season. Both friend and foe, winter is a true dichotomy.

The winter that I gathered the material for this painting was mild with little snow. Mid March was ravaged by a blizzard that blew for days. The storm abated, I hiked out on my snowshoes on a warm, cloudy day to see the snow melt. Large patches of ground were already laid bare by the rapid advance of spring and there was a musty, earthy fragrance in the wind. A lone fox track emerged from the woods and crossed a snowbound field. A few days later, the track and all the snow had melted in pools and freshets, making their way to swell the rivers already overflowing with spring run-off.

Red Fox Walking

Sketch of Fox and Hare

Red Fox Running

SNOWSHOE HARE

The Snowshoe or Varying Hare, as he is also known, changes the colour of his coat to match the seasons – brownish grey with light underparts in summer and white in the winter, except for the black tips on his ears. As the days grow shorter in the fall, the fur begins to turn white, not from the cold, but as a direct result of diminishing light. The thick hair grown on the feet completely obliterates the footpads and allows the hare to travel easily on top of the snow – hence the name 'Snowshoe.'

Varying hares follow a unique population cycle lasting 10 years. At their peak it is common to see a number of them together at once, but as the population reaches its zenith, disease and food shortages affect them so severely as to almost exterminate them. This begins a new cycle, but meanwhile other animals, notably the Canada Lynx, which rely heavily on hares for food, experience lean years when they cannot adequately provide for their offspring. In turn their population is reduced.

In my area, Snowshoes seem to prefer low, swampy places. Well-worn paths criss-cross their territory in winter, making their presence obvious, but not their whereabouts. Relying more on camouflage than cover, each hare selects favourite, dry hide-outs or 'forms' as they are called, where they stay until dark when they come out to feed. Vegetarians, they prefer succulent grasses and plants in summer; bark, buds and dried plants in winter. One curious, but vital habit of the hare is his ability to consume his own scat, deriving the remaining nutrition in a severe winter.

It is nearly impossible to see a Snowshoe in the snow unless he moves. I love this ghost-like quality which is so elusive and difficult to reproduce in a painting. White on white was, to me, a real challenge which I resolved by adding just a touch of sunlight. The resulting shadows help to delineate the animal and show him as an entity separate from the snow. The fallen apple tree and milkweed plants provide a suitable background design.

Snowshoe Hare

TIGER WITH KILL

Most of my pictures centre around the animals native to North America, primarily those near my home. A raucous old crow or tiny chickadee is every bit as exciting to me as, in this instance, a tiger. Of course, big cats do have a dynamic charm which is hard to ignore and I never turn down an opportunity to portray one.

This painting is not representative of the body of my work, but is one in which I was interested because of its inherent difficulties. The large cats, in action or defensive postures, have been done often in sporting illustrations. They may suffer from overexposure and be considered somewhat trite by certain art critics.

In my view, subject matter does not affect artistic excellence or importance. If I have succeeded in making a fresh statement and communicated it to others, then I have done what I intended. Only time will tell whether any of my pictures deserve to live as works of art.

Other animal painters, Bob Kuhn in particular, have dealt with big cats very effectively and it was with them in mind that I approached this picture. By burying the buffalo carcass in the grass, most of the gore was eliminated. The tiger's defensive snarl has been reduced to a surly grimace. The threat is there but the big fellow has lots of confidence and the muscle, if necessary, to fend off would-be trespassers. I left it to the viewer to guess at what or whom the tiger is growling.

Tiger with Kill

WAPITI

I well remember the first wild elk or *wapiti* I ever saw. I was on a train bound from Vancouver to Calgary. We were passing through Banff National Park and the sun was low, colouring the mountain tops a brilliant orange, chilling the valley with cool green, blue and purple. As we sped along the Bow River, I beheld one of the most spectacular sights of my life. A huge bull elk standing in the water raised his head to watch the train go by, water trickling from his chin. What a wonderful setting – but it didn't last long. The train just kept on rolling. I resolved to go back to the mountains – on foot if necessary, but never again on the train.

That experience was, I suppose, the genesis of this painting. The dramatic light on the mountains, the elk in the cool valley, almost dwarfed by their surroundings. Elk are, in my opinion, the most handsome of the deer family. I've seen hundreds of them in the wild and I've listened to them bugle and fight as I laid around a camp at night. They are great lusty mammals full of primeval vigour. I'll make a large finished painting of this some day and hope to capture just a portion of the excitement one can only experience fully by being there.

Wapiti

WAPITI - Dec. 18/60

WHITE-TAILED DEER WITH FAWNS

Woodlots provide protective cover for myriad varieties of wildlife, which despite hoards of mosquitoes in summer, lure me to wander through them, slapping and cursing as I go. Bugs and bad weather are not fun but extensive field experience and careful observation is what makes a painting live. Although I sometimes use my camera to whisk me through these unpleasantries, as I did in this instance, I use it only as a tool for recording specific information, which I am not bound to, but which I can use or change as each situation demands. The light effects and likewise the control and orchestration of the composition are my own. The deer are naturals in this setting and help to promote the mood I wanted to convey of tenderness and tranquillity. Warm patches of sunlight filtering through the thick foliage brighten an otherwise cool picture.

Because my major interest in painting lies not in the theatrical, but rather the neglected, subtle beauty we so often overlook, it was with great affection that I painted the almost perfectly camouflaged fawns. The intimacy of the moment is the element I like most to catch.

White-tailed deer are fairly common mammals and they prosper in settings where the woods are broken by fields and there is a good water supply – an accurate description of Sydenham Township where I live. The hardwood bush on the adjoining farm to mine provided the habitat for my deer as it has, in varying degrees, for other pictures.

Now and then, I tackle a project that I know will take much time and patience. It took me a year before I was satisfied with the doe and fawns. The secret is that on completion the finished work should show no trace of the troubles occurring in its development.

White-tailed Deer with Fawns

White-tailed Doe Reclining

SELECTED BIBLIOGRAPHY

ALDROVANDUS, ULYSSIS. *Ornithologiae* Bologna, 1637
ANKER, JOHN. *Bird Books and Bird Art* Levin & Munksgaard, Copenhagen, 1938
AUDUBON, JOHN JAMES. *Birds of America* London, 1828, 4 volumes
AUDUBON, JOHN JAMES and BACHMAN, THE REV. JOHN. *Viviparous Quadrupeds of North America* Philadelphia, 1845-48
BARBARA, LYNN, *The Heyday of Natural History* Jonathan Cape, Ltd., London, 1980
BOWDLER-SHARP, R. *Analytical Index to the Works of the the late John Gould,* F.R.S. Henry Sotheran & Co., London, 1893
CATSBY, MARK. *The Natural History of Carolina, Florida and the Bahama Islands* London, 1731, 2 volumes
EDWARDS, GEORGE. *Gleanings of Natural History* London, 1758, 3 volumes
FUERTES, LOUIS AGASSIZ. *Album of Abyssinian Birds and Mammals* The Field Museum, Chicago, 1930
GESNER, CONRAD. *Historiae Animalium* Christopher Froschoverum, Tiguri, 1555
GREENEWALT, CRAWFORD. *Hummingbirds* American Museum of Natural History, New York, 1960

HILL, MARTHA. 'Liljefors of Sweden, The Peerless Eye,' *Audubon* Magazine, New York, September 1978
HILLS, ROBERT. *Etchings of Quadrupeds, Comprising Rudiments of Drawing and Numerous Series of Groups for the Embellishing of Landscape Scenery* London, 1806-15, 7 volumes
JACKSON, C.E. *Bird Illustrators* Witherby, London, 1975
KURTH, DR WILLI. *The Complete Woodcuts of Albrecht Dürer* privately printed, n.d. (ca. 1930)
LANK, D.M. *Animals in Art – An Introduction* Royal Ontario Museum, Toronto, 1975
LANK, D.M. *Four Centuries of Animal Art in Books* Federation of Ontario Naturalists, 1979
LEHMANN, JOHN. *Edward Lear and his World* Thames & Hudson, London and New York, 1977
(LEONARDO DA VINCI). Reynal & Co., New York, 1956
LILFORD, LORD. *Birds of the British Isles* Porter, London, 1885-97, 7 volumes
LILJEFORS, BRUNO. *Det Vildas Rike* Albert Bonniers, Stockholm, n.d. (1941)
MUNSELL, A.H. *A Color Notation* The Munsell Color Company, Boston, 1919
NORELLI, MARTINA. *American Wildlife Painting* Watson-Guptill, New York, 1975
PALMER, A.H. *The Life of Joseph Wolf* Longmans Green & Company, London and New York, 1895

PLINY, CAIUS. *The Historie of the World: Commonly Called The Naturall Historie of C. Plinius Secundus* Adam Islip, London, 1634
PRIESTLY, J.B. *Victoria's Heyday* Heinemann, London, 1972
RIVIER, LOUIS. *Le Peintre Paul Robert* Delachaux et Niestlé, Neuchatel and Paris, n.d. (1928)
ROBERT, LÉO-PAUL. *Les Oiseaux de Chez-Nous* Delachaux et Niestlé, Neuchatel and Paris, n.d. (1933)
RUSSOW, DR K.E. *Bruno Liljefors – An Appreciation* C.E. Fritze, Stockholm, 1929
SKIRA, ALBERT (Publisher). *The Great Centuries of Painting* Various Authors, 21 volumes. 1955 et seq.
THAYER, ABBOTT. *Concealing Coloration in the Animal Kingdom* The Macmillan Company, New York, 1909
WAETZOLDT, WILHELM. *Dürer and his Times* Phaidon Press, London, n.d. (1955)
WILSON, ALEXANDER. *American Ornithology* New York and Philadelphia, 1829
WILTON, ANDREW. *British Watercolours 1750 – 1850* Phaidon Press, Oxford, 1978
WOLF, JOSEPH. *Zoological Sketches* London, 1866 and 1867, 2 volumes

General Editor
JEREMY BROWN

Editors
CATHERINE MUNRO
INGRID PHILIPP COOK

Produced by
SUSAN BARRABLE

Designed by
HELEN MAH at
THE DRAGON'S EYE PRESS

Colour separations
GRAPHIC LITHO-PLATE INC.

Printed by
BRADBURY TAMBLYN & BOORNE LTD

Bound by
T. H. BEST PRINTING CO. LTD

Typeset in Caslon 74 by
TECHNI PROCESS LIMITED